HOW IT ALL HAPPENED

The Raw Truth

SAMUEL P. HOLLOWAY III

ISBN: 978-0-692-33750-9

10 9 8 7 6 5 4 3 2 1

Visit my website at

www.SamuelHolloway3.com

DEDICATION

I would like to dedicate this book to #26. I never knew what I had until it was gone. Sometimes we step into relationships while we are hurting from a previous relationship and end up hurting the ones that truly love us and have our best interest at hand. This is exactly what I had done to #26. I can't say I am sorry enough. The saying is true, "Hurt people hurt people!" I hurt you like I had been hurt and I am so sorry from the bottom of my heart. I love you!

I dedicate this book posthumously to Terrence Kelly, Former Professor of Atlanta Metropolitan State College. He helped me catch the errors within my book, "Eyes Without A Face." He helped me with some of the work in my college courses and made sure that I was on track to succeed. He became a very close friend of mine. Mr. Kelly departed this life in December of 2014. He will be greatly missed!

I also would like to dedicate this book to my mother. I want her to know that I love her despite her actions. I love her more than she'll ever know. I would climb down a lion's throat and I am sure that he would eat me. I would fight a snake and I am sure he would bite me. I would swim the deepest sea and I can't even swim.

I would walk through fire and I am sure to get burned. I say all this because there is no love greater than I have for my mother. *Eyes Without A Face,* and *How It All Happened~ The Raw Truth* are not books to bash my mother nor have people hate her. These books were written so other parents could learn from my mother's mistakes. I love my mother!

Finally, I dedicate this book to anyone who has HIV or AIDS, lost someone to the battle from the complications of HIV or AIDS, and me.

I thank GOD for giving me the strength and courage for allowing me to put my story and status out there, and for being able to be vulnerable and transparent.

I feel totally accomplished and like I did what I was created to do — helping to tell the story for the unheard voices. I am just one of the many voices behind the book because it actually happened to me; however, my story may be yours too!

ACKNOWLEDGEMENTS

I want to give the utmost and highest respect to my Lord and savior Jesus Christ. I know that without you, none of this would have been possible.

I want to give thanks to my family and friends. Those of you who have stood by me strong; I hold you all very close to my heart.

I want to extend a special thanks to all of my fans and followers. Without your support, this could not have happened.

Last but not least to Myron Schippers, Richard "Rajheem" Williams, Wilhelmina Hampton Smith, Artist Paul J. Harris, Damion Snowden, Shantel Floyd & Demond Goode; you all made a very emotional impact on my life…

Thank you

The Beginning

By Demond Goode

You have read my story
Everyone can see the scars
Written all over my body
Beaten by the people
Who you would think
Would instinctively protect me
Molested, finding my REAL FATHER
Something good is ALWAYS followed
With something bad in my life
Selling my body for material possessions
Because a 9 to 5 and school was not cutting it
Eventually making it a lucrative investment
My body was my temple and also
My money making machine
And did it do me well.
Finding love, getting married
Best moments of my life
Then blackened by a love gone all wrong
And almost killed for the love
I had for the man I called my husband
Shattered, torn, misused
Left to die by the man I made vows with
Who claimed he would never hurt me
And now living with HIV
You would think life would be simple now
But glance into my world
Look into my eyes and see all
That I have seen
I've told my story, my life is as it may be
I've lived long after I truly died
I am *"Eyes Without a Face"*
And this is *"How It All Happened."*

INTRODUCTION

S ome people may wonder why I wrote this book in great detail about some men that I had sexual encounters with. Some people may look at me like I'm a sex addict, however, that is not the case. Being molested, raped and abused, some people come forth when the time is right for them. In my case, three years ago was the right time, because I almost lost my life and felt that I was going to die with my story inside of me. I couldn't speak in great detail about the sexual encounters that I had with my molesters. I could speak about the first encounter, but others well, I some things are better left unsaid.

It wasn't until I went to speak to a Psychiatrist about my issues that I was able and ready to face my fears. I didn't understand how the men that had sex with me as a child shaped my understanding of what I looked for in a man today. My counselor said that most people live with the after effects that I experience today and I was not the only person with these emotions and feelings. All of the seven men that molested me (not including two of my second cousins that had sex with me), and by Bernard raping me had a lot to do with the men I picked.

No one ever gets over being abused sexually. That is a type of abuse that comes into your mind more than anyone knows. I've never harbored any feelings of anger towards them for their sexual encounters on me. I loved them through those times and I still love them today. It's not the type of love that I have for #26. I was a 10 year old child when those things started and I felt unloved and unwanted and was looking for love and attention and found it within my molesters. At that time I didn't know that what they were doing was actually wrong.

Educating others isn't going to be easy. It's hard to describe to some people that when someone is kidnapped or molested as a child, it takes over a child's mind. A child that has been through the things I went through falls in love with their abusers. It's kind of like this; the child that's being abused is told over and over how much they are loved by their abusers. With time, the child begins to believe them. I was that child that believed my molesters loved me. All of them didn't say that they loved me, but the attention that was shown to me made me believe they did.

When I express the fact that my molesters shaped the man that I want to today, it's because I left with parts of them that I still want. Alex left me wanting a man with a nice looking penis that's circumcised. Munk left me wanting a man that is aggressive. Michael left me wanting a man that is hairy. Stacey left me wanting a man that is tall. Coop left me wanting a man that is bowlegged. Double G left me wanting a man that has pretty feet. Anthony left me not wanting a man who is uncircumcised. My two second cousins Coop, and Bernard my rapist, left me not wanting a dark man at all. My cousins were my cousins, Coop placed a gun to my head, Bernard raped me and they were all dark skin.

It was hard for me to leave those parts of them because as a child growing up, I loved them. I still didn't see anything wrong with what they had done being a teenager. I bragged to some of my friends because I had felt like I was just turning out the boys in the hood. I would have no clue going forward that their actions would live with me forever.

This book will captivate your attention. It's a journey into my life of acrobats on steroids. The book is informative, educational and spiritual. Come look into the eyes of my abusers. Here's why I wrote about my abusers in great detail. What I wrote about happens more than we think. It happens daily and most people just sweep this issue right under the rug as if it doesn't even exist. Some people will say we shouldn't revisit the past because it can bring back bad memories. I've learned that by not going back to the past, you can never get to your future of being happy and you would never understand the current problems that exist. I had a very hard time understanding what is written here until I sought help. Writing this book became my coping mechanism because we all cope with things in different ways. Without seeking help, I wouldn't understand "How It All Happened" either!

TABLE OF CONTENTS

PROLOGUE

You know my cycle; something good is always followed by something bad. If being molested, beaten by my mother and brother, finding my real father, being shot, raped, stabbed, escorting and almost killed from someone that was in love with my husband wasn't enough; I'm now living with HIV and my body is fighting another infection, this one in my mouth from the wire that held my teeth together. And to top that off, my ex publisher was trying to fuck and extort me throughout this entire process — LITERALLY.

CHAPTER 1

THE NAUGHTY PUBLISHER

The things that kept reoccurring in my life began when I became a victim at eight years old. Being a victim is the dysfunctional way that I have lived my life longing for love I've never found.

It was so easy for Price to walk into my life and put his arms around me and take advantage of me. My publisher being the sociopath that he is, just like Price, he saw me as an easy target. This is a cycle that has to end with me. It has almost cost me my life. All this time while I was searching for love, it was my mother's love that I was searching for but never found. I was yearning for my biological father's love and approval but never received it unconditionally.

I was terrified of having a meaningful and trustworthy relationship because I was actually scared of myself. Reckless behavior and promiscuity had always been an easy way out for me. I needed love and protection and I coped by exploiting and divulging myself. I never received the love that I needed and felt I deserved. I'm still learning to love myself.

✶✶✶✶✶✶

When I first met this publisher, he resembled the Gay Father that raped me in my book, *Eyes Without A Face*, but he was different in lots of ways. I met him through Facebook and a mutual friend named Tanisha who's in his book club. She told me that she knew he would be interested in my book because of the books he's written as well as those he's published and that I should meet him. She suggested we become friends and I hit him up as soon as he accepted my friend request. From there he asked me about a mini synopsis of my book, which I sent it to him through an email. He then asked for my number and after emailing it, he called. We chatted a bit before he decided we should meet at Starbucks next to "Bulldogs Gay Night Club" in midtown Atlanta.

I brought my rough draft manuscript along with me and once we were there, I ordered a caramel Frappuccino while he read through it. He loved it right away and wanted to publish it. He said there were numerous errors that needed to be corrected before he could publish it since he published only the best books. I agreed and told him that I would work diligently along with him and the team to get the book completed to his liking. He then started to go over the price, rights and what comes with his contract.

The publisher's contract was $2,500, which included copyright, publishing, formatting, book cover, artwork, photo shoot, editing, ISBN, barcode, promotional flyers, speaking engagements, website, voice and diction lessons, etc. ... Mina, my first publisher was helping me for free. I had heard so many stories of people being taken by phony publishers, so I was kind of hesitant at first. After we met, I called my sister Teresa to discuss his contract and legal matters. She was my go to person when it came to money although I felt I could do it myself I needed a second opinion, especially when it came to my book. She told me to go ahead and just be careful and double read everything and triple read if I have to, and then contact a lawyer.

The publisher and I agreed to meet the next day at his condo in downtown Atlanta. He told me to bring several outfits and my checkbook when we met. Once I arrived, we met in the conference room of his building. It was beautiful with plush white leather furniture and other accessories that could have come from CB4 furniture store in Atlanta, which is very expensive. The room was magnificent. I was totally impressed; there was even a water fountain in the breezeway. As we went through the contract, I told him that I didn't want to pay $2,500, because I still needed to have two more surgeries and Texas Crimes Compensation hadn't paid for some things yet. I was still coming out of my pocket paying my dental bills and I didn't want to screw myself in the end.

He told me that was not a problem and he totally understood where I was coming from. He said he could definitely work something out with me to lower the cost and charged me $2,000 instead. I then wrote him a check for $2,000 and he initialed the contract and crossed off the $2,500.

He said his photographer was out sick but he did photography too, so he would do the photo shoot. After I gave him the check, he started to look at my outfits. He then picked out two outfits for me to wear for the first round of pictures. The fountain pose was one of my first shots. It was perfect and I loved it after he showed me.

Then that ever-familiar look came into his eyes. I saw it right then and there he looked like my molester Bob and the Gay Father that raped me, Bernard. I was immediately uncomfortable but kept going. I knew that this could not be happening to me all over again. *WHAT THE FUCK?!* I thought to myself.

The weather was so beautiful outside for an August day in Atlanta; maybe even about 85 degrees. The publisher then instructed me, "Go through the doors to go inside the building."

I said, "First, what about my things?"

He said, "Boy, look where we are, your things are fine." He then entered his code into the door keypad for his loft and we went in. We started up the stairs and stopped just shy of the second flight in the emergency stairwell and he said, "This would be a beautiful picture. Take your clothes off."

I was like, "*WHAT?*"

He said, "Boy take yo damn clothes off. I have seen more dick than you will ever know, plus I just gave you a bomb ass deal."

I thought about it for a minute, and thought *Hell, I've fucked for money before,* and I was desperate, so instantly that prostitution mode kicked in and I stripped. Before I knew it, I was butt-ass naked in the emergency stairwell. Anyone could have come down the stairs at any moment, but honestly, I didn't give a fuck. The only thing I was thinking was getting my book out and I didn't have to fuck, get fucked or suck any dick to do it. So there I was naked, posing my ass off at every angle. After he virtually got his rocks off (he didn't actually touch himself) by looking and taking pictures, he told me to get dressed and we continued our photo shoot.

I felt kind of odd and awkward afterwards but like I said, I thought about my book being published and instantly that thought was gone just like the thought of me getting fucked for money. I was back in money mode and whatever needed to be done, I was going to do; to a certain extent this time around though.

A couple of days later around 11 pm, the publisher called me, and he sounded very excited. He'd uploaded all the pictures to his computer and was ready for me to see the one he had picked as the

Bio Picture for my book. He wanted me to come over right away so I could be taken away in awe as he was. Of course I was hyped as hell. This was a picture that was going to be shown everywhere to represent my book and me.

I jumped my ass in "Accomplished" (my car) and sped up 75 North to his loft. Words can't express the way I felt at that moment. Now in the back of head, I knew it was late at night and his freaky ass would probably try something. I wasn't worried because I had mace and a stun gun. Let his ass get out of hand and he was going to be fucked up because I wasn't playing that shit.

As I entered his loft it was dimly lit with just the TV on. He was sitting in the front room with the laptop open. We sat down and he pulled the table closer to us. When I looked at the laptop, I was immediately shocked to say the least. It was full of dicks! All kinds of dicks! Just men with their dicks out! Young and old. "As young as 16," according to him and "as old as 40."

I was thinking like, *Are you fucking crazy, I know you didn't have me come over here for this!*

He saw the look on my face and said, "Close your eyes, you too young for that."

Bitch you wanted me to see that, is what I thought and wanted to say, but I just laughed. In the back of my mind I said, *This mother fucker is a pedophile and maybe even a child molester, too!*

He then opened a file that contained other peoples' files. Ones I assumed he was working with too. He then went to my file and opened it. He went through the pictures and then said, "POW! This is the picture that I want to use to brand you." He said, "Your dick should be rock hard right about now!"

He was wrong, my dick wasn't hard but the picture was very hard to say the least. I was sitting in front of the water fountain and

I was looking up thanking GOD for getting me to that point. That was actually the very first shot he took.

After that, we discussed the cover concepts and how that process went. Then he offered me a drink. By that time it was around 1am. I said, "I'm good," but I wanted to say, "Hell naw Bitch!" I then tried to end the meeting when he offered to smoke some weed with me but I would have to roll it. He knew I wasn't going to pass that up, so I stayed. I know, stupid!

We smoked, watched a little TV and talked about my book. He told me how I was going to be a millionaire. I wouldn't have a worry in this world after my book hits the shelves. Then he pulled the plate out. *Um, isn't that cocaine? I thought? I know this Bitch is not about to do a line in front of me. Oh snap, this bitch just did not one but a couple lines. WTF!!!*

"You want some?"

"I'm cool, just weed for me."

"You know if this ever gets out, I will quit working with you and give you back all your money."

"Dude, that's your business."

After a while and him doing a couple more lines of coke, I left. I was totally taken aback by this whole ordeal and called my sister Teresa the next morning. I had given this bastard my money already and he was snorting coke. I know that's his business but he even went to the extent to offer me some. Did I look like a fucking cokehead to him or something? I was going crazy. My sister told me to just make sure I keep it totally professional with him and don't go over anymore at night.

After that, things went rather smoothly, or so I thought. Then things started falling apart. The publisher's team members were all leaving him one by one. Everyone was saying how he wasn't paying them on time and sometimes not at all.

******

Before long, I had sent the final payment for my books to be printed, which was around $1,000 total. The printing of my books had been prolonged since we had agreed on an October release date. I paid for the balance of my books December 9th and found out two weeks later that my first shipment would be split. *SPLIT? WHY? HOW?*

The publisher's reply was, "It's the end of the year, the holidays, and the printing company is backed up. Don't worry, you will have the first part of the shipment of books by December 15th to fill the orders that you already have through your pre-sales. The second half of books will be to you before January 5, 2012 of the New Year."

Of course that was a lie. December 15th passed and this motherfucker went on vacation. *Are you fucking kidding me?* I thought to myself and even screamed out loud! He was truly trying to take advantage of me and I knew it. But I wasn't going to allow him to steal my joy or my dream. I've come too far to let this bastard take everything that I've worked so hard to get. So I played the role with him.

Once he got back to Atlanta from his so-called vacation, he continued with sending me sexually explicit text messages asking for RAW sex. I continued to say that I would give him what he wanted once my entire contract was met.

Finally on December 27, 2011, I received my first shipment of books, but to make matters worse, they came with 63 errors that were supposed to have been corrected when I paid him three times during the formatting process. Plus, the copyright page was not in my book. Go figure! He wanted more money to fix the errors and said that I was covered with the copyright issue because I had sent myself the "Poor man's" copyright by mailing myself my manuscript and not opening it.

After I mailed off the books I had, I was still in need of books to fill orders because I had pre-sold more than the amount of books I received. The publisher told me I would have the rest of my shipment by January 5th of the New Year, 2012. January 5th came and went with no books.

I then began to have interviews from the radio and television stations and everyone wanted me to bring books to the interviews. The only problem was that I had no books to bring to the table. The publisher promised that once my first interview was scheduled, which was February 9, 2012, "you will have books in hand."

My first interview was in Minneapolis and it was a TV and radio interview with Mr. Flowers from MPNS television network. He wanted me to bring a total of 50 books with me to the interview. I told the publisher and he said to just go ahead and go to Minneapolis. He would have the books mailed to an address there where I could receive them. I believed him and went to the interview and drove to Minneapolis bookless.

Once I was there, he told me that the books would come late but I could just let the network know and they could still purchase the books. I did the television interview, cancelled the radio interview, and still, no damn books. Finally he told me that the books would come late and would be delivered to his home in Atlanta by the 17th of February. "Are you fucking serious?" was my reply.

Of course this bitch had nothing to say besides, he was sorry and he would pay for the lost sales. Once I got back to Atlanta, I had the flu from the weather change of 60 degrees to -20. He was still sending explicit text messages asking for sex throughout this entire time and I was still saying I would have sex with him unprotected because he had my damn product.

The publisher sent me the delivery tracking number from FedEx and the books arrived on February 17, 2012 along with another set of books that he was promoting. I went over to his house even though I was sick, and this bastard still wanted to have raw sex knowing I was sick and had HIV.

After I told him I couldn't because I was too damn sick he allowed me to take my books and I left. I knew that day that our contract was going to be over and done with. I was ready to fire his ass that fucking day and a lawsuit was coming very soon.

CHAPTER 2

THE LOST BUT NOT FORGOTTEN

My nephew and sister played a major role in my life. I hadn't seen either in years and it was time to reconnect. The last time I saw my nephew DeAndre, he was only three years old; walking, talking and so full of love. As a child, it really didn't have an effect on me being an uncle as it does today. The one thing about him that stood out to me as a teenager was my nephew saying, "Chips." He loved potato chips more than anything.

I wanted to find my nephew so badly. I wanted to find my nephew because I wanted him to have the love and the support that I didn't have when I was growing up. I wanted him to know his father's side of the family just like his sister's. Everyone in our family would ask questions regarding DeAndre and I never could give them any answers. I didn't know where he was or even what he looked like. All I knew was his mother had left Gary, Indiana and vanished without a trace. She didn't call or write to let us know where she'd moved to.

I began to think more about my nephew as the time went by. I often wondered if he was okay and if he was thinking of us also. I thought about him a lot for a while and finally decided that it was time to do something to kill my curiosity. In June of 2001, I began to write to different organizations to help find lost children. After that became a dead end, I decided to go back to square one; Gary, Indiana. I went back to the house where they once lived. The new residents gave me my first clue. They said the last they heard was that the family had moved to California.

Then I began calling information and giving them Tia's full name. Unfortunately I hit another dead end. Information had no listings for Tia and the ones that they did have were not available to the public. Then one day in October of 2003 while I was talking to a lady at work, I began telling her about my nephew. She told me that I should try and go through the Salvation Army. She mentioned that it would cost me though. I didn't care, money was not an issue for the price of finding DeAndre.

I had written the Salvation Army in October and two months later they finally responded. I responded back as soon as I received their letter. I thought I ran into another roadblock after their first response. They informed me that DeAndre was a minor and they did not search for minors but they could search for the parents of the minor. My mother, being a big help at this point provided me with important information that the Salvation Army had requested in order to proceed with the search. They asked for the full name, date of birth, place of birth, and any other information I could provide for them {DeAndre and Tia}. I had all the information they asked for and much more.

My mother had a friend that worked in the Welfare Department in Gary and she gave my mother, Tia's mother and DeAndre's information. Finally it felt like I was making progress. All the while I was searching for DeAndre I was keeping everyone around me informed. This was when my brother and I had started to build a closer relationship with each other. Then on March 2, 2004 the Salvation Army responded but all they could tell me was that Tia had indeed lived in California. I already knew that so once again I felt like I was not getting anywhere.

Then I broke down; I just couldn't take it any longer. I cried to the receptionist on the phone from the Salvation Army and she gave me a number and an address in Washington DC, Social Security Administration Department. I called the number and I got a lady on the phone that understood exactly where I was coming from. Thank GOD she had a heart.

Even though she didn't give me the location of where I could find my nephew, she gave me the correct name of his mother and the city in which she resided. Tia had gotten married so the name that I had given to information was no help. I called information back and the number was unavailable. After receiving Tia's new legal name, I again reached out to the Salvation Army to try and get more information about my nephew. While writing them, I paid my fee for the third time, I wrote them seeking help and I knew the amount that I would get back would be priceless. Seeing my nephew meant everything to me. I wanted him to know his family and wanted our side of the family to know him.

I then went to work and sent an "All Staff" email to find anyone who could help me locate my nephew. I was working for the Credit Union that has several different locations and about 500 employees. I was desperate and could have lost my job but received huge information on how to look for people. We conducted a Google and Zaba search with no luck. I had almost given up all hope of ever finding my nephew.

On April 27, 2004, I received a call on my cell phone while I was at work. I was just walking into the vault room of the credit union and my phone began ringing. An unfamiliar number showed up with a 916 area code. Hello!? Then the lady asked me, "Are you Samuel?" I said, "Yes?" She said, "I'm not sure who you are, but the Salvation Army said that you were looking for me, my name is Tia."

I immediately started screaming and crying and I fell to my knees. I thanked God, I was so happy; I had finally found my nephew. Words can never express the way I felt that day. My heart was racing with joy. I told her who I was and that I'd been searching for her for over two years, now my search was finally over. She told me that before they had moved she was trying to contact us, but we had moved away too. We exchanged numbers and then we hung up.

I immediately called my mother and we cried together on the phone. Ironically my brother called my mother from jail and she told him the good news. The word was around the family that I had finally found DeAndre. I made a promise to myself that I would find him and I truly did it. Although it took me over two years it seemed like a lifetime. Later that night I called Tia back and she let me talk to DeAndre. I didn't know where to begin because I was so happy. I tried my best to hold back my tears while I was talking to him, but I couldn't. After speaking with him that night I started writing my nephew a letter to let him know that we have always loved him and were looking for him. I didn't want him to think that his father or his father's family had abandoned him in any way. I wanted him to know that he has always been in our hearts.

I gathered a bunch of pictures of just about every family member and made a scrapbook for my nephew. I had pictures of everyone down to his grandfather's obituary. I put names by all the pictures and explained what was going on at that time in the picture, and even the year it was taken. I made special pages as well of his siblings and of myself. I also made pages of his grandmother, great aunts, uncles and cousins.

I think what hurts the most is that I have yet to meet my nephew. It's been many years since I found him and we are still in the planning stage of when he can visit. It seems there's always some type of situations that delays us from seeing each other. But by the grace of God, when my brother was released from prison, my mother sent him to see his son.

Tia sent my brother some pictures of DeAndre before he left to go visit and to all of our surprise, my nephew looks like a split image of me. Everyone said it's because of the hell my brother had put me through that his seed turned out to look like me. We look just like twins when you put his picture against mine. Now my nephew is 22 years old, and married with two baby girls whom I've yet to meet.

******

After my mother had, had Romie at the age of 14, she was pregnant again within six weeks. My brother and the new baby wouldn't even be a year apart and my mom wasn't even sixteen let alone, she was still in high school. My grandmother wasn't allowing that in her house because she had five other kids and worked the midnight shift. My grandmother also had other grandchildren at the time. My grandmother gave my mother a choice. But it was more like an ultimatum.

My mom would have to give her unborn child up for adoption, get an abortion, pick which child to give away or move out of her mother's home. After giving birth to Teresa, my mom brought her home and with the help of her sister Sylvia tried her best to care for my sister. Unfortunately she was not able to, and my aunt Sylvia had even asked to drop out of school to help but my grandmother said no.

My mother went to her Aunt Lillian, who's my grandfather's sister. My mother asked her if she could leave her baby daughter with her until she was able to finish high school. Being that my great aunt was having problems conceiving she was eager to raise my sister and give her back to my mom when my mom was able to care for her. My mother, not really knowing what to do and being so young gave my great aunt her child at six months old. The agreement was for my mother to graduate from high school, get a job, a place to live and then get her daughter back.

At first it seemed like the perfect plan but my great aunt had something else in place. My Great Aunt Lillian and Uncle Leotis lived in Maywood, Illinois with lucrative careers, a nice home, and beautiful cars. They were raising my sister as their own child and before long my mother was disallowed to see her. You would have thought that being she was the only child with two parents who worked she'd have the perfect life but later as adults we discovered that was not the case.

My great aunt initially brought my sister back and forth from Maywood to Gary to see my mother, then it all stopped abruptly. My great aunt had a change of plans that my mother would have no clue of until it was too late. My mother and aunt Sylvia went to Chicago to try and take back her child only to have my great aunt and uncle go out of town down south to Mississippi or that's what they were told.

That was the story they told every time my mom came to get her child back to avoid giving her back. My mother was not allowed to see her child any longer after that until years to follow. I would be nine years old before I would even see my sister for the first time that I could remember. I had always been told that I had an older sister who looked like my brothers twin. My sister and I are five years apart, my brother and I are six years apart and my brother and sister are just eleven months apart. Our birthdays fell in January, February and December.

When I was nine years old my great aunt brought my sister to meet us in the projects in Gary. It was the beginning of nightfall when a big white Cadillac pulled up in front of my Aunt Denise's apartment in the projects and they stepped out; my great aunt, uncle and my sister. I was so afraid of my aunt after the stories I'd heard. To me she was the devil carrying a pistol and I didn't want to even get close to her but she called me over. "Lil Robert, come over here and see your sister," she said out loud. All the kids in the projects ran over because I had spoken of this beautiful image so much and no one believed me that we indeed had a sister out there. Plus there was this big white pretty car out in the projects and everyone wanted to know who was in it.

I ran up to this tall brown skinned girl with long curly hair. She was beautiful with an infectious smile and she was my long lost sister. The fervent hug we shared stayed with me forever and all she said was I love you. After we all went into my Aunt Denise's apartment, I just looked at her in amazement. I didn't want to leave her side nor did I want her to leave mine. This was around the time that my mom was dating Bob. I was craving love and attention and in a just a few moments my sister had shown me that.

After some brief visits back and forth to Gary, my aunt allowed my sister Teresa to spend some weekends with us. It didn't last long but I enjoyed the time we had. My sister was famous for making us salads. She would make the salad for my brother and I, and she would feed me. My mother still managed not to be around much this time. We had no food in the house so we ate from my aunt's house or my sister would spend her own money.

After a while, my sister had stopped coming to visit and I had no clue as to why. Suddenly my great aunt passed away in April of 1989. There was talk of my sister coming to live with us, but things changed so fast that she never came. Instead she went with my granddad's other sister that lived in Chicago as well. This was kind of perfect as my mother went back and forth to Chicago quite often to see my sister. I eventually got the chance to even start spending the weekend with her and my cousin Pumpkin. They lived there together with my aunt Ruthie Mae and Uncle Buddy.

Pumpkin was Uncle Buddy's granddaughter and now she and Teresa were being raised like sisters. I was happy because I had two girls in my life that adored me and took me everywhere with them. Things changed as my sister had gotten a little older. She and my aunt had, had a disagreement and my aunt called my mother. That was the worst mistake ever. My mother and I raced over to Chicago and I was hoping that my mother would not flip out on my sister like she did with me.

My mother entered my aunt's home, she didn't even say anything to my sister and she started taking off her coat and jewelry. My aunt was telling my mom how disrespectful my sister had been and my mother began to yell at my sister. My sister then started yelling back, screaming at my mom telling her how she didn't raise her and she was never around, then came the ultimate insult before I could even say anything "You aren't my mother no way." My mother struck my sister hitting her in her face with her fist. They were fighting in the kitchen as my sister struck my mother back. My aunt was in the background telling my sister not to hit her mother and respect her while my sister was yelling for someone to get my mother off her. As I tried to help my sister, my uncle Buddy pulled me back. I just stood there and cried as I watched my mother attack my sister. That night I was able to stay there with my sister as my mother drove back to Gary alone. I didn't want to leave her side as I knew the pain she was feeling. After that, my sister and aunt's relationship changed for the worst.

Some time passed and my dad (Robert) drove to Chicago and got my sister. He brought us all together; my brother, sister and myself under one roof in August of 1992. That would only last for so long until my mom accused my sister of having sex with my dad so she had to leave. The next few times I saw my sister were on bad terms; at funerals. In 1996 when my grandfather passed away, in 1999 when her father passed away and in 2001 when I was stranded in Mexico during the attacks on 9/11, which would be the last time I'd see my sister until July of 2008. During that time she'd gotten married and had two daughters.

In July of 2008, my aunt Teresa passed away, she was my mother's baby sister and my sister shared her middle name. My sister hadn't seen the family in over 10 years and we hadn't seen each other in 7. The family gathered at the church for the wake of Aunt Teresa and as family hour began I was looking for my little cousin Nina, while texting her I looked up and spotted a lady who resembled my sister from behind. I thought to myself, no that's not my sister and I put my head back down and kept texting. Something said look up again and as soon as I did, we caught each other's eyes. I jumped up out my seat and dropped my phone and ran to my sister. We hugged and cried out loud. It had been 7 whole years since I'd seen my only sister.

Once again, I felt that childhood feeling of not wanting to let her go. As they walked us to the other room I was still crying very loud. Then my brother came and joined us and we all cried together. My mother never came to the circle. After being seated and going through the wait, the pastor asked if anyone had any words. My sister got up and began to speak. She's a minister and her husband's a pastor and the way that she spoke sent chills up my spine.

She began to sing with that beautiful amazing voice, her first song was, "I won't complain." I was immediately in tears hearing her sing that song. Then she went on to sing, "Going up yonder," at that point I was taken away. I couldn't stop crying as her angelic voice touched me and moved everyone in the church. I wish that my aunt had gotten the chance to see my sister. Throughout my life, I've seen my sister about 10 times that we've counted. The bittersweet thing about her is that she's a spitting image of our mother.

CHAPTER 3

MY RISKY LIFESTYLE

Looking back at my life, I can honestly say I have taken some risky chances. Even if I didn't feel that I was born gay, Bob {my molester} and the Down Low (DL) men made that choice for me. I had no say so in the matter I just did what I was told. Eventually those men would shape my lust for straight men today. I had been looking for love and my judgment was so fucked up. I was just blind. Not having that parents love the way a child should has left me as open prey and I would have to survive life to understand that.

I had no idea what the hell a condom was or how to even use one. Especially when I was a child having sex. I was 13 years old when I first tested the waters and had sex with a girl.

She was the neighborhood whore and she didn't even stay in the neighborhood. I guess I wanted to prove that I was still a man to others and she wanted me bad so I did it. I can't really say that I liked it, it was totally different being that I was now in control of the situation.

I didn't hesitate once the opportunity presented itself although we were not physically ready for what was about to transpire. Neither one of us had protection. Remember, she was the neighborhood whore and I had been getting fucked by boys since I was 10 years old.

While having sex, I felt nothing in relation to wanting to be with her. I was just trying to prove a point and making sure she walked away with something good to say.

The very next day I didn't think anything about it or her until I went to take a piss. "What The Fuck!" The head of my penis was dripping something that looked like blood and semen mixed together only slimier and I thought the burning sensation was going to kill me.

I didn't know what to think, as this has never happened to me before. So I went next door not wanting to tell my aunt or my mother what I was feeling because I didn't know what the hell it was. Nay Nay and Boobie stayed next door and they were the neighborhood street pharmacists. They had it sewed up and not to mention, the neighborhood whore was their little cousin.

I told them what I was experiencing and they immediately said, "That bitch burnt you with her nasty ass!" I didn't give a fuck, what happened; I just wanted this shit to go away. Every time I took a piss, I nearly died; honestly, I thought my dick was going to catch fire.

Nay Nay took me to the Public Health Department on 5th Ave in Gary. She acted like she was my sister so I could be seen being that I was under 18 years old. The nurse there gave me some pills, told me I had Gonorrhea and that it would take up to 14 days to clear up. Wow, I had to actually wait 14 days, and then I would be back to normal!

But the neighborhood whore left telling everyone, "That boy fuck so good, he can't be gay and his dick was so big I wanted to make him my man. Even better, I had heard, it was the best dick she ever had had and she had slept with one of my cousins. LMAO

******

While I was getting fucked by my 2nd cousins and the boys in the projects from the ages of 10 through 19 right before I left Gary in December of 1998 moving to Minneapolis, Minnesota; I had never used a condom. I didn't even know how to use a condom let alone have the courage to tell the boys to put one on. Every boy that I had sex with from that time came inside of me or on my ass. Most of them came inside me and when I was giving head, all of them came in my mouth; some I had to swallow because I was forced, and some I didn't.

And throughout it all, I still remained HIV Negative.

******

When I was escorting, I practiced safe sex to the max. I brought my own condoms even though they were provided. I didn't trust anyone when it came down to sex and money. I protected myself in both categories at all times. My new boss (the pimp) was even more protective when it came to us wearing condoms. He serviced the white-collar, married society and didn't want a bad reputation, which would hurt his business. The Boss stressed the importance of HIV/AIDS knowledge and it was during this time that I became acutely aware of its importance

Please don't forget, I was raped by someone who had Full Blown AIDS and I was married to someone that was HIV Positive. I got involved with a young man named Adonis. He was a sexy,

DL, bowlegged, yellow-bone who was an absolute dream and I figured with him having two children and being in a serious relationship with his fiancée I let my guard down. To be quite honest, after the second time of having sex with him, we never used a condom again. I knew he had a fiancée, but they were having issues and sex was one of them, they were not having it. I figured I would be safe with him being that he had already had two healthy looking children. All while Adonis and I were together, we both tested negative at the local Red Door Clinic in Minnesota.

I still remained HIV negative throughout that relationship and even afterwards.

Price on the other hand was a different story. From day one we had unprotected sex. He was fine as hell and I felt that he really was feeling me so I allowed myself to have raw sex with him. Hell, we didn't even think of asking each other our status until the next morning and that was after he had ejaculated inside of me the night before. The only reason that we ended up even talking about HIV was because Lucciano had left a message on Price phone and Price played the message on speakerphone.

The message said in a very sarcastic tone, "Bitch, you think you doing something. That's why I left you with something that it will make you so sick to your stomach that you will want to go and kill yourself!" Price had the nerves to ask me what I thought he was talking about. I told him that he needed to go get tested and if he had known if Lucciano was HIV Positive. He said then that it didn't matter because they always used a condom. I would learn later that they NEVER used a condom. But of course, it was too late to be asking anything.

I was so in love with Price from day one that my judgment on the whole HIV issue was fucked up. I was blind to the fact. Not me.

I was invincible to this disease. Furthermore, Price was too fine to be Positive. Yeah, that's how I thought, that someone would have to look sick for them to be Positive and he didn't fit the description of a HIV person at all.

******

While I was prostituting, I had over 2,000 sexual encounters with men and women. I knew never to go out of town to meet a trick that I had never met before but I did after some occasions meet them without the Boss's knowledge. I was all about making money and I'd creep on many different weekends. I was living a dangerous life but I didn't care because money was the only thing that was on my mind. I wanted it and I was willing to do anything and I do mean anything to get it. Anything except raw sex, with a trick that is. I didn't trust them like that but I had some trust in them.

My clientele were mostly Caucasian men and women. I can count on two hands how many of my tricks were African-American. My counter parts had African-Americans on their team but it seemed like all the Caucasian's were requesting me. I know for a fact it was because of what I brought to the table which was my 10' dick. Whether they were getting fucked, fucking me or playing with my dick, they wanted me and that's all that mattered.

******

I remember this like it was yesterday. I was 20 years old and it was November of 2000. It was right before Thanksgiving and in the beginning of my career as an "Escort." I had met a guy through my cousins Felicia and Cookie. The guy was Felicia's baby father's cousin. Cookie liked him but they said he had gay tendencies and wanted me to find out if he was really gay. "He was a bad boy and did everything the bad boy's did but he just had them tendencies," Felicia said. Robert you always told us what to look out for and we do. **Bad boy means thuggish or drug dealer**

Sometimes when we're out eating or something, he's always looking at men in their face very hard like he wants them, looking at them after they walk past and the way he shook one man's hand and looked in his face. He is GAY! Watch what we say as they screamed out laughing saying it together at the same time.

They gave me a good description of him and said his name and age. His name was Ricki and he was 27 years old. Hhhmmm, he was 7 years older than me; I was just 20 at the time and being that I was doing what I was doing, I liked older men and to top it off he was a "bad boy."

The next time I saw Ricki was when he came over with his cousin Marcel to visit Felicia at Uncle Kenny's house. Uncle Kenny's house was the place to be because everyone was always over there. We would be in the living room watching movies on the 60' screen TV with surround sound, smoking the best weed because that's all Uncle Kenny liked to smoke and sometimes drinking. That particular day, all my cousins were there from Troy, Stanky, Fatboy, to Uncle Kenny's kids; 5 to be exact, remember he has 10 kids.

All the boys were in the living room watching TV, and the girls and I were in the kitchen watching the other TV while my auntie was cooking. Uncle Kenny came into the kitchen and passed Nina one of the blunts that was going around, he said "Hey y'all, Marcel's cousin is gay!" We all just busted out laughing and he walked out the swing door and went back into the living room without uttering another word. My partner in crime Nina gave me the look and I was already on it.

Of course that really intrigued me. Without hesitation, I got up out of my seat immediately and exited the kitchen through the swing door into the living room. I then sat right next to Uncle Kenny, which was on the opposite end of Ricki but right in front of him on the black leather sectional couch.

I got the blunt coming my way from Ricki and we locked eyes right then and there. It was like everyone was in their own zone as we engaged in small talk; everyone except uncle Kenny that was. **Side Stare** I saw him in my peripheral vision looking at us.

"So you Robert huh?"

I smiled and said, "Yeah, how you know?"

In my mind I already knew. Marcel had probably told him that his baby mother Felicia had a gay cousin that was on his shit. I was living with uncle Kenny at the time but just about to move out and I had just bought a new car, was in college, had 2 jobs {everyone thought} and I was always flossing the newest shit. I had it so I splurged on myself and my cousins, too.

"We should get up and smoke" he said.

"Fasho," I replied.

"Take down my number."

Just like that, I took his number down and exited the room like nothing ever happened and went back into the kitchen with the girls. I didn't say a word but I gave Nina that look for her to follow me into the bedroom and I broke it to her that I was getting up with Ricki later on that night. We died laughing to ourselves so Felicia and them couldn't hear us. Although they put me on to him, I had to remember that Cookie, my cousin by marriage, liked him but she still thought he was gay. I wanted to know for sure before I told them anything. Well to be honest, I wanted him first before I told anything.

He was mad attractive. He wasn't my type by skin tone because he was dark like chocolate but his body definition was killing the game. He was 5'9", just an inch taller than me; cocky football player build weighing around 190 pounds solid and bow legged. I loved bowlegged men because of Coop, plus I really loved the way that he looked at me. He looked at me like he wanted me to be more than just a fuck and I wanted more than just a fuck from him. He was a bad boy doing bad boy things and I was strictly in money mode and I knew if I worked what I had I could have more than what I wanted.

Meeting up with Ricki that night was exciting and risky. We met in the back of Uncle Kenny house after midnight when he pulled his car next to mine. Surprisingly he wasn't trying to hide the fact that we were meeting up; after all, what straight man wants to be seen with someone who's gay unless they're comfortable with their own sexuality?

Once we pulled off after he asked me to follow him and he got into my new Neon, he said the words that I felt was coming. "Hey man, don't tell nobody we be getting up."

And just like that, I already knew what type of party this was and I was about to use it to my advantage. I was not going to be just walking away with a wet ass or giving some nigga random head and I get nothing in return. I wasn't going for that at all so I began to ask all type of questions. I knew what I needed to hear to make me either want to continue kicking with him or simply walk away after that night. Remember, I was escorting so there was nothing that he could do for me on a money tip, it would have just been some hood dick that's black that I wasn't engaging in at the moment. I had no time for broke ass nigga's what so ever. I was all about my paper and if you didn't have it, you didn't have me either.

I asked about how he made his money, did he have a girlfriend, did she have a job, any kids, and was that his car, where he stayed, family in Minnesota and who he hung around? He said he didn't work, he sold drugs and robbed people for their drugs, he had a girlfriend and they lived together, and had a daughter who was 5 years old. They had been together for over 7 years. That was his car and she worked and gave him her check. Damn, he had her in check like that I thought immediately. They stayed in south Minneapolis and he had family there but most of his family was back home from Gary. WOW, he was Gary too? Small world.

After a couple of months Ricki and I were like Broke Back Mountain. I knew everything about him I thought that I needed to know. I stayed with him for about 7 months. He was indeed a down low brother. The first time we had sex was at the Hilton Hotel after the weekend of my 21st birthday when I returned from out of town with Jonathan. He had it all planned out and I was over taken because he was so thuggish and a bad boy.

The room had a Jacuzzi and he had weed and drank and did both before we engaged in a hot steamy shower were we washed each other's body. After we were done showering, he picked me up and walked me into the bedroom laid me on the bed and placed my legs in between his head and went to town. Damn, our first time having sex and he was making me fall in love. Yea right, nicca where the money at, I was used to this but not used to this. I was loving this though at the moment.

All while he was eating me, I was just thinking about the size of his dick. DAMN, that nicca had every bit of 9" thick with a hard curve to the right and a fat head. I was nervous but ready; I wanted it. After all, I was only having sex with white men and I was over taking them. I felt like a power bottom because after having been screwed one night by the below average size dick at first, one dick wasn't just enough. They were always generally around 6 or 7" rarely would I run into a white man with 8" or more and never have I come across one that was bigger than mine, so I was ready for Ricki to say the least. I wanted a challenge.

After he ate me out for about 30 minutes like he was at the local soup kitchen, he pulled out a magnum and placed it on his dick. Whoa, it looked so pretty and the condom still looked tight. Look just like mine when I put a condom on, I thought, just with a curve. He put some lube on my asshole and on his dick and worked his way in. Ricki did more than rock my world that night, I was hooked and so was he.

By mid-February of 2001, Uncle Kenny was getting very sick but was still doing his thing of riding around town with his friends. I was at Kmart shopping for my new apartment because I was about to move at the beginning of the month with Ricki. Ricki wanted to furnish it and I was not about to say no of course. By this time, I was working at the Credit Union and escorting. Ricki and I were walking down an aisle and he was placing things in the cart and uncle Kenny walked past. He looked directly at us and said, "Oh, I'm telling and bursted out laughing and walked away!"

To my surprise once again, Ricki didn't even care. We simply went on shopping like nothing ever happened then after he dropped me off back at Uncle Kenny's house, everyone was over. I walked in and everyone was laughing and saying that they knew that Ricki and I was messing around. I didn't say anything nor did I deny anything. I didn't want to mess things up that I had going on.

By this time, I was getting half of his girlfriend's check because when she got paid, he got the check and started cashing it through my account and I kept half and gave him back half, plus he was giving me money on the side of his sales. Then to top that off, he was supplying me with weed, "Hydro" to say the least and he had just furnished my entire bedroom, dish set and bathroom. I wasn't ready to mess any of that up just yet. I knew that if he had something to hide and something to loose then he definitely had a lot to give and I was ready to receive.

******

After uncle Kenny died and I was raped, Ricki's girlfriend found out about us. I had called Ricki's cell phone one night but his girlfriend answered and asked me all type of questions, "Why was I calling him so late, who was I, did I drive the white Neon, was I gay and was I fucking her man?" WTF. I snapped out on her to say the least because she was snotty and fag came up somewhere in that conversation out her mouth.

I hadn't been gone from Gary that long and the projects was still in me. I told that bitch, I was calling for Ricki because we were supposed to be kicking it that night and I had changed my plans to do it, my name was Robert, I drove the Neon, yes I'm gay and I am fucking yo man, now what?!

She went into a rage before Ricki snatched the phone from her and told me he was on his way. Once he got to my house, I lied and said she was lying after he said I told her that I was fucking him. Bitch please; she wasn't about to mess up my money. I had gotten out of character with her and had to quickly jump back in with him.

We went on like nothing ever happened until this bitch came to my job at the Credit Union. She walks in calling me all types of fags and the receptionist had called the police before I could even get from around the teller line. Of course, I wasn't going to fight her right there and I honestly don't know what I was going to do but I was going to do something.

The police came within seconds because they were parked outside. This was the City and County Federal Credit Union so police were always there. They escorted her off the premises and I filed a police report. This bitch was bad I thought. She had the nerve to actually come to my job to fight me over a nigga. She stupid as hell. Her man was DL and she was wanting to fight me and still stay with him.

Needless to say, that same damn night, my cousins Nina, Troy, Felicia, Cookie and lot of friends went out to the bowling alley and Anika, Ricki's girlfriend was there with her friends. Once she spotted me she came over talking shit. Before I could get a word out, Nina had checked her so hard and Troy told her if she stepped up he was going to knock her ass down. This damn girl was 6 feet tall and built like a man. I wasn't scared but I knew if I hit her, it was going to be over because I was going her have to hurt her and go to jail. Minnesota didn't play that putting your hands on a woman.

Eventually all that died down after a month or two. Ricki had to say something to her or my cousins had put the fear of fire in her because she never said anything to me again after that night and we bumped into each other a couple of times after that at random places like the gas station or at the grocery stores.

******

By June, Ricki and his friends were about to take a trip to Florida. He needed a rental car but didn't have a credit card so I rented the car for him under my name using my credit card. That night before I rented the car and when he asked me to rent it, him and I went to go make a sting. We picked up some white guy on

35th and Park Ave over in south Minneapolis. Before the guy got into the car, Ricki told me not to look at the dude and just keep looking forward. I was cool with that, I didn't need to be getting caught up in any of his bullshit.

I took them to someone's house about a couple blocks away and when he was getting out, Ricki told me to turn the car facing the street and turn the lights off. I did just that and he came out alone about 10 minutes later carrying a duffle bag. We ended up at Mystic Lake Casino and Hotel that night. He had all types of weed, drank and money. He hooked me up on the weed and gave me $2,000.00 and said when he gets back from Florida, he would hook me up some more. I knew that he had just robbed somebody because he didn't go in that house with a bag.

******

While Ricki was in Florida and I was at work one day at the Credit Union and Minneapolis Police showed up at my job and wanted to talk to me in a closed room. My boss told me to use her office and they began to question me. My heart was all over the damn place because I was dumbfounded with no clue to what was going on.

Apparently, Ricki had robbed and killed someone and I was under investigation as the getaway car driver. I started talking like water running faster coming out the faucet. I was not going to jail for any dude and I didn't have anything to do with nothing. I told them what I knew which was mostly really nothing besides we had picked up a white man and I never saw his face, I took them to a house, turned my car facing the street like I was told and kept it running and 10 minutes later Ricki came out the house with a bag.

He had a gun with him and we went to the hotel afterwards and had mad sex and that's all I knew which was the total truth.

They said they believed me and would need me to testify against him and asked if I had known where he was at. I said okay and I sure did, he was in Florida in my rental car and was supposed to be returning later on that week.

Before I could even call Ricki, Florida police was calling me. This motherfucker had just robbed a bank in Florida, hit a woman trying to run from the police and they had arrested him but the rental car was totaled out in the accident. OMG, my world had just turned upside down. Then to top that off, Ricki called me from jail and told me not to tell the police anything. He had already spoken to Anika and the murder was on Minneapolis news with his picture as a wanted fugitive.

Ricki was extradited back to Minneapolis and faced trial. He was so mad at me because I was a witness against him but I wasn't about to go down for him, he wasn't my man. Unfortunately he beat the murder case because I was not a good witness because I really knew nothing and the white man that we picked up was a crack head and just a decoy to get into the house and there were no other witnesses. This bastard just got off with murder. I wasn't scared but I was pissed.

Furthermore, I was now being sued by the lady he had hit in Florida. The rental car that he tore up was over my comprehensive limit, so the company was coming after me for the balance because I didn't add the extra insurance on when I rented the car so I took his ass to court and sued him for the total amount that the people were suing me for and to have the liens against me taken off and placed on him. I WON! But the bitch never paid me!

Marcel was killed a few months later after all that and I never saw Ricki again.

******

In the same process of dealing with Ricki, I had met Greg. Greg and my cousin Nina were in the beginning stages of talking to each other. But my girl cousins were on point when it came to spotting out a DL brother. Nina came to me one day and asked what I thought about Greg.

Greg was beyond fine as hell I told her. That boy had a body to die for with an 8 pack. He played basketball for Washburn High School and was a senior along with Nina. He had hazel eyes, bow-legged of course and a red bone. Every time he licked his lips I had pictured him licking my ass but never went after him because my cousin was feeling him.

It wasn't until one day sitting in the living room talking about my new place that uncle Kenny and Nina brought up Greg. Greg can help you move your things out the basement that Ricki brought, Nina said, being that I needed help during the day moving and Ricki was out making stings. But most of all, she said, I need you to come on to him to see if he gets down. Uncle Kenny said, "that boy is gay, you can't see that Nina?"

We all just died laughing and Nina was like, "Daddy for real?" Uncle Kenny said, "He be staring at your cousin every time he comes over." I was shocked but kind of felt it but I didn't really think it. Uncle Kenny said the perfect plan would be for him to help Robert move and see what happens after that.

It was on after that. Greg came over later that night and we were all getting high in the living room watching TV and Nina asked Greg would he help me move. He said for sure without any hesitation and asked what time did I need him. Before I could say anything, Nina said just come over after traffic that way y'all won't have to sit on the highway too long being that Robert is moving to West St. Paul. He said cool and that he would be over tomorrow to help me load the car up.

I called Slumber Land the next day and made arrangements for them to deliver my new bedroom set that Ricki purchased. It was everything I had wanted. I had a black canopy bed along with the dresser, headboard, chest and mirror with the box spring and queen size mattress. I wanted them to come earlier that day and I met them there with my first load of things. After they set it up, I went back to Uncle Kenny's and arrived there by 5 pm.

Right on time, Greg was there by 7 pm. It was already turning night and West St. Paul was a good 40 minutes from uncle Kenny's house in south Minneapolis. I'm glad it was a Friday that I moved because while driving Greg said, you're not going to want to drive me back home after were done. I thought, "I'm about to turn this boy out." I said you might be right but who knows?

When we exited the highway off Roberts St. exit we drove past a liquor store and both of our brains must have thought the same thing and we both said something about the liquor store at the same time then we laughed so I grabbed a pint of Hennessey and on to the house we went. After unloading the car and putting everything up, it was well after midnight. Greg was right, because I was tired as hell and I didn't want to drive him back home then drive back home myself.

He'd brought some weed so we started drinking and smoking and listening to the radio because my cable wasn't hooked up yet. About an hour or so later, Greg asked did I have any flicks. My dick instantly got hard as I said yep and popped one in. I had straight and gay flicks, I was well prepared.

While watching the straight flick, he laid across my bed and took his shirt off. He then said man, this shit got my dick on brick. Me following his lead I replied, "Mines too." Then he just stood up and dropped his pants right in front of me. He said, "When the last time you had a dick in your mouth and started dangling his dick across my lips while I sat on the edge of the bed. I then went to town and started sucking his dick right then and there. He had his hands on the polls of the canopy and started swinging back and forth with his dick in my mouth.

Then he proceeded to tell me to take my clothes off and he started taking his off. He stripped butt ass naked from socks and all. I was ready than a mother fucker. This dude had a dick on him. Not big as mine but he had dick and I wanted it. All while I was licking and kissing his body, I was thinking of Ricki and my cousin Nina. I couldn't get hard for shit in the world to save my life. Then Greg started sucking my dick and I was there in no time at all.

Greg threw me completely off when he laid across my bed on his back and threw his legs up with his ass in the air and said, "gone head and lick my hole like my uncle do!" WHAT, I said out loud. He knew I wasn't going and he put his legs down and started sucking me again. I said let's just jack off. In my mind, I was thinking not only is this mother fucker DL, but he was getting fucked by his uncle too. After we both jacked off we feel asleep naked on my new bed under the covers.

The next morning waking up, he didn't say a word about last night and I didn't either. The ride back home was deadly silent. The radio played the entire time without us speaking to each other.

After I pulled up to his house, we shook hands and he got out the car.

I went straight to uncle Kenny's and told Nina and Uncle Kenny and Uncle Kenny said, "I told you that boy was gay." I felt bad because my cousin said she really liked him but also glad we set that shit up so she wouldn't have to find out later if they started dating. We never told Greg that we knew he was gay or that I had him. That was Nina and my secret but she stopped talking to him in that way and he never questioned why.

As for our relationship, we carried it on and off until about 2006. I never saw Greg again until late 2009 when Price was working at one of fly by night jobs at Wells Fargo in Brooklyn Park as a Teller. Greg was a member service representative and offered to help me.

OMG, I thought when I first walked in and saw him. I had just purchased my new 2009 Mitsubishi Gallant and wanted to show Price. I walked in and Price was on the Teller line and Greg was in the lobby. He told me to come into his office before I could even say anything. He was so excited to see me and I was even more excited to see him. He had grown over the years into an even more beautiful brother.

He was every bit of 180 pounds solid, skin looking so soft, and I was lost in his waves. I had to snap back and turn around to see if Price was looking at me because Greg's office was just right in front of the Teller line. Sure enough, Price had a customer but he was looking and looking hard. I knew I had to get out of there and get out of there quick.

I cut Greg right off mid-sentence and told him I was married and that was my husband on the Teller line. Greg started laughing and taunted me which pissed me off. He said "Damn, he just a Teller and he's a girl, when you become a straight top?" I was floored because he knew the lingo but I was pissed off because he had just called my husband a girl. Had he seen something that I hadn't? **Message**

Anyway, after he said that, I left from out of his glass cubicle but not without giving him my business card first, being that I was the Branch Manager at my bank. **Side Stare** I had to show him what I was doing and plus I did want him to call. I was going through it with Price and I had thought about cheating.

Price didn't say anything about what he'd seen once I arrived at his window and we carried on and I asked him could he step out and see the new car. When Price got home he blew up. He let me know that Greg told him about us and that he knew me after he asked Price if we were married. Then Greg told Price that he and I went way back and started laughing. That pissed Price off and I told him what happened and that, that was before his time. He didn't care though and told me that, that nicca bet not start calling me because he also had known that I gave him my business card.

Greg really tried to do me in. He really went the extra mile to tell my husband all of this information and I never released his. Fucking bastard! I was heated and vowed to fuck him up on site if I saw him. My relationship was already going nowhere why would he try to take us there even quicker?

A couple of days later Greg called my job and I let his ass have it. He said "I don't fuck with Price like that and I can't believe that you went and got a little kid like him?" so he was jealous. He said that everything about him was bigger and better and I stooped below my means with Price. I told him, "Fuck you!" and I just hung up. I never heard from him and he never called my job again.

CHAPTER 4

LIVING WITH HIV

Three in five Gay men in major U.S. cities are living with HIV/AIDS. What's even more astonishing is that half of them don't even know it. I had always thought that HIV was spread mostly through homosexuals because that's what I had always heard however according to the CDC, HIV worldwide is transmitted mostly through heterosexual contact. Of all the tough decisions I had to make in my life, disclosing that I am HIV Positive to the world was probably the hardest. I felt all types of emotions charging through my body when I learned of my status.

My feelings ranged from suicide, blame, fear, guilt, depression, and loneliness to anger and shame. Then, I could hear people, well gay men saying that, "He has the package, he is sickly, and his T Cells are low" and that set me off. I began asking myself, "Why me?" I was truly afraid for my life; "This" was a "Death Sentence."

I thank GOD every day for allowing my feet to touch the floor. Afterwards I head to the bathroom for my regular routine, I am forced to walk past that mirror and when I see myself; I know I love Samuel Holloway although in the back of my mind, I see that guy who's a carrier of HIV. No matter how many times I walk away or turn to see myself at a different angle, I still see that guy with HIV. GOD is keeping me here for a reason so I am going to make the best of it.

You know the saying; "What doesn't kill you makes you stronger." Trust, HIV has not killed me it just makes me more aware of the decisions that I need make in my life going forward. This book will help you to see how I carry myself with HIV, how others perceive me, how you can contract it, ways to keep yourself healthy and to clear up many myths that most people believe.

I thought I was invincible and believed "It could never happen to me." Yeah right! Ironically this is the one thing my mother always talked about when I was a teenager. I can hear her now in the back of my mind sometimes to this very day, "You're gonna catch AIDS you faggot!" OMG, now I have brought life to her prediction or shall I say curse. I was infected with the non-curable and sometimes deadly virus. I have "The Package," or "The Monster" or whatever it is unless there's a major medical breakthrough it's not going anywhere any time soon, I'm stuck with it.

I only had sex with DL MEN so I felt that I was untouchable. For the most part, we always protected ourselves so I didn't worry.

Adonis was different, I'd only used a condom with him one time. He had a fiancee' and they'd just had a baby so I trusted him. I could almost pin point when I contracted the virus but I don't want to point any fingers at anyone. No one placed a gun to my head and made me have unprotected sex. I was a grown man and I could have asked potential partners for their status or I could have gone with them to get tested before sex; but who really does that now a days?

It could have been all the DL MEN from the projects or my second cousins....none of them used a condom. It could have been Bernard my rapist who ejaculated in me. It could have been Adonis; all I know is what he told me which is he was STD free. It could've even been Gary. Price and I did that 3 way relationship with him and he came inside of me to.

There were too many people and too many examples of how I had risky sex to pin point who actually passed it to me. Many times I was careful, but I was often risky. After I found out my status, I educated myself about the disease, I knew prevention was too late for me but I quickly learned that I can still live a normal healthy life and enjoy sex without infecting my partners. I asked my doctors a multitude of questions and even called in after my office visits. I was shell shocked. I wanted to know what this virus was, what it would do and how I could fight and beat it? I wanted to live and I was going to find out everything I needed to know, "By any means necessary," and I wanted to help educate others about it in the process too.

******

There is a difference between HIV/AIDS. First we have to get tested to know our status and the difference between HIV/AIDS. Most people are afraid to get tested for fear of knowing an unfavorable status, so they don't. In the end, that only hurts them. If you find out too late then the disease has probably become deadly. An early diagnoses can prevent you from having the AIDS diagnosis and can help you keep your CD4 count high and viral load low.

The most commonly used HIV tests available are oral tests and blood tests. Oral tests use a non-invasive swab to collect cells from the inside of the mouth and can provide a result in 20 minutes.

Blood tests use a sample of blood, either from a finger prick or a larger sample often drawn by a needle from an inner arm and generally takes a few weeks to come back from the lab.

Most HIV tests check for antibodies that the body produces once infected. It can take as long as three to six months after exposure for these antibodies to be measurable on a test. During this time, you could test negative for HIV but still be infected and able to transmit the virus to others. It is important to get re-tested at least six months after exposure to confirm diagnosis and get tested continually every three months going forward.

To set aside all myths about how you can contract HIV I have decided to list them because most people don't really know. The five ways to catch HIV is only through certain body fluids; Blood, Vaginal fluids, Breast milk, Semen (cum), Pre-seminal fluid (pre cum) and rectal (anal) mucous. You can't catch HIV through using a toilet seat, shaking hands, hugging or kissing unless there's a cut inside the mouth or on the lip. HIV can not be spread by sharing food, drinks, eating utensils, computers, telephones and other common items. You will not get HIV from donating blood however recent studies lists some mosquito bites as culprits.

I did not know that all condoms are not equally good at stopping HIV transmission. Nor did I know that some people have been able to totally get rid of the HIV virus in their bodies by taking their medication. Other body fluids and waste products-like feces, nasal fluid, saliva, sweat, tears, urine, or vomit, don't contain enough HIV to infect you, unless they have blood mixed in them and you have significant and direct contact with them.

If you test positive, there is a difference between the two diagnoses. HIV and AIDS are totally different. HIV is when your CD4+ count is above 200. Most states go by this guide line. Once your

CD4+ drops below 200, then you are considered to have AIDS. Once diagnosed with AIDS you will never go back to the HIV status again. Although your count may rise again, you will live the rest of your life in AIDS status. The normal range that a person infected with the virus should be in is 500. Your CD4+ cell count can tell you about the strength of your immune system.

500 is normal, 200-500 is weakened, -200 is severely weakened.

You want to ensure that your T Cells are up and your viral load down. You want to be considered Undetectable. 100k copies is a high viral load, 10/30k copies is a low viral load, 40-75 copies are undetectable.

***Lucciano's count was below 20 when I visited him at the hospital in West Virginia. He looked to me how I had imagined a person dying from the disease would look.**

Since the start of the epidemic, gay and bisexual men have been severely affected by HIV/AIDS. Today, more than half of all new infections are among men who have sex with men (MSM), the only risk group for which new infections are on the rise. While anyone gay or straight, who has unprotected sex or shares needles is at risk for HIV, the large numbers of HIV among MSM means a high propensity of being exposed with each sexual encounter.

We all know there is currently no cure for HIV/AIDS yet many of us still carry teams of sexual partners minimizing the aftermath. There is no vaccine to prevent HIV nor cure for those of us who are already infected, but there are medications that help people living with the virus live longer and healthier lives. For someone who is HIV positive, it is important to know as soon as possible to determine the best treatment.

******

Living with HIV and the effect of the robbery that occurred November 2, 2010 in Dallas, Texas was another traumatizing blow for me. I was set back into a depressing stage. I had already been diagnosed with depression a few years earlier but I had it under control. Not only did I look bad but I felt even worse and my health was declining fast. I had lost well over 20 pounds from being on a liquid diet for over 8 months. Before the robbery my T Cell count was 800+ which dropped drastically to 344 and my viral load was well over 13,000 copies. I was now HIV detectable but I still didn't have AIDS. THANK GOD FOR THAT...

After the robbery, I was immediately diagnosed with PTSD (Post Traumatic Stress Disorder). One might have thought that I had fought in someone's war based on how antsy I'd become. The symptoms were all over the place and I didn't even know it. I had a phobia of going outside at night alone, going to gas stations any time of the day and people walking up on me and even worst walking behind me. I was having anxiety attacks often and thought I was going crazy.

It wasn't until after moving to Atlanta and speaking with my doctor and telling her my symptoms that she diagnosed me as PTSD. My doctor and Physical Therapist both told me that I would be paralyzed on the right side of my body and my hand would never be the same again. I would not be able to run, pick up anything over 40 to 50 pounds without hurting myself and the scars will last me a lifetime.

But within a few months of continuous physical therapy, praying all the time, keeping my faith, exercising on my own with a squeeze ball for my hand and walking around my apartment complex for a couple of months straight, I regained 100 percent use of everything contrary to what they predicted. I was determined! I wanted my life back. GOD restored me to good health.

When I went back to visit the doctor in March of 2012, I was ready, willing and able to show my Therapist what I could do. She gave me the ball and told me to squeeze it like I normally did but I could never fully squeeze that ball. This time I squeezed that ball so hard I thought it would pop and it was sponge. She told me to run to the other end of the room. Usually, I would take a couple of steps and stop in between but on that particular day, I ran like I was running in the Olympics and even ran back to her without stopping. She said, pick up the 25 pound dumbbells with both hands. I not only picked them up but curled those bad boys about 20 times in each hand before I put them down.

GOD definitely showed up and showed out that day. My doctor, some nurses and my Therapist were all in the room and we all cried together and hugged one another. I told them I couldn't have done any of this without GOD and their assistance.

I'd shown tremendous progress yet I still had one problem, I was addicted to the pills that were prescribed to me. I was using Vicodin, Zoloft, Ambien, and Xanex. I was prescribed those right after the incident. All I had to do was say that I was in pain and just like magic, I had more pills. My doctors knew I had pain but I don't think they really understood the extent of my pain. It wasn't like there was a test to be performed or anything but the way I went in for visits they bought into it.

I was popping anywhere from 12 to 16 pills a day. I was taking anywhere from 4 to 5 Vicadin, 2 to 3 Zoloft, 1 to 2 Ambien and 3 to 4 Xanex and my 1 Atripla (HIV pill) every day. In addition to that I was smoking weed, cigarettes, Black & Mild's and sometimes drinking alcohol. I could have killed myself but in the state of mind

I was in, I don't think I really cared. I just wanted to keep feeling the way I felt, HIGH and pain free!

I felt like my body was in one place but my mind was some place on the other side of town. I felt numb to almost everything. I had no pain, hurt or emotions. It was very hard for me to cry. I was just angry as hell. I wanted to kill someone some day's because I didn't know what emotion to follow.

I started reading the Bible somewhat and had prayer sessions with my sister and friends without telling them what was wrong with me. I had already been through so much and I didn't want to continue to burden any of them with my issues. I began to meditate on my own once again. I thought about my family and my nieces, nephew and great niece. My dream was to see all of them grow up to adulthood. I knew if I kept taking the pills I would eventually kill myself. It took the passing of Whitney Houston for me to want to take charge of my own life. She was a wake up call.

I thought to myself, shit just got real. I didn't know of any of my peers or family members dying from prescription pills but I did know of a many celebrities that did like Michael Jackson, Anna Nicole Smith, Gerald Levert, Heath Ledger, and Whitney Houston.

I didn't want that for me so I prayed and I prayed and I meditated hard. I set a date that I was going to stop taking the pills cold turkey. I stuck by my word and on April 21, 2012, sure enough, after taking 1 more Vicadin and 1 more Xanex I flushed every remaining pill down the toilet. I kept my faith and HE never left me. From that day forward I took the words wouldn't, couldn't and can't out of my vocabulary and replaced them with "I CAN" and "ANYTHING IS POSSIBLE" I'm possible!

******

HIV/AIDS comes in all forms; big, small, tall, short, smart, dumb, rich, poor, wealthy, ALL RACES, cute and ugly...It has no face. HIV does not discriminate. It looks just like you, me and any other normal person. You can't tell if someone has it by looking at them. I've learned through time and visiting the clinic that sometimes you will never know who has it. Just because someone is skinny or gay does not mean that they have HIV.

The first time I walked into the clinic in Cobb County, GA, I lost it. Literally! I couldn't believe what I had walked into. I saw all types of people, people that I would've never thought were infected with the virus but they had it. Most of the people in the clinic sitting in the 14 chairs that lined the walls of the office on both sides were mainly women; African American women. There were a few brothers too but I can honestly say out of the 14 people in their, 10 of them were women.

Some of the women were gorgeous. Some had toddlers, babies in strollers and a few were even pregnant. Their ages ranged from about their late teens to elderly women. I wanted to make sure I was in the right place so in a whisper I asked the desk receptionist if I were in the right place or not and she told me that I was in the HIV clinic waiting room. I concluded that everyone in there had what I had and that's when I lost it; I couldn't believe my eyes. Some of those women were so beautiful though. I was in a state of simultaneous intrigue, hurt and anger at the same time. As I sat there with tears rolling down my face, I couldn't even hide my emotional pain if I tried.

I felt obligated to talk to those sisters to see what the hell happened to them and how they caught this horrible illness. I was pissed. One girl was a model and if she was on the streets, I would never have picked her as a person that had it. These women were tall, short, big boned, skinny, slender, dark skin, light skin young and old. Age wise and appearance they represented a conglomeration of my sisters, cousins and my family members.

I stepped out to gather my composure. While outside I decided to called my cousin Felicia and come clean. I brought clarity to the lie that my mother had already told my family. I wanted to make sure that they would not have to sit in the seat that I was sitting in. I didn't want to be there but my health was more important. Felicia let me know that she was behind me 100% when I was ready. I told her once I return to Minneapolis I'd make sure she gathered the family because I wanted everyone to know; it was not a secret any longer. I knew this disease had to stop and it would have to start with me making it happen.

That day inside the clinic I saw the many faces of HIV which prompted me to become a Peer Educator so I could help more people become aware about the disease. I started taking weekly classes and got certified. Sometimes it made me cry just listening to the many stories of how others became infected. It was more devastating when I learned how some put their trust into others without being tested together before having unprotected sex.

Like I stated in the beginning of this book, I had all kinds of emotions when I first learned of my positive diagnosis, I was devastated. I've always wanted children and I just knew after testing positive that, that would now just be a figment of my past dreams.

After speaking with my doctor and doing research, I've learned that my dream can still become a reality. The process is called, "Sperm Cleansing." The only thing is, the process is very expensive which would have to be followed by injecting the sperm into a female (Artificial Insemination).

******

There are six different classes of HIV medicines. Some are injected by needle, some are liquid, and the rest are either pills or capsules. Some people have to take numerous combinations to keep their HIV under control. Fortunately, I only take one. The goal of all HIV medicines is to prevent HIV from making copies, so that the amount of the virus in your body stays low and your CD4+ cell count stays high.

*****

The cost of the pills are very expensive and most people can not afford to pay for them out of pocket. I thank GOD that I am covered for my medication under the Ryan White program. Otherwise I would definitely be sick if not dead by now. A thirty day supply of my pills cost around $1,500.00 a bottle. Think about taking this pill every day for the rest of your life with no insurance or not being covered under programs like ADAP (AID'S Drug Assistance Program) or the Ryan White program. It costs around $18,000.00 a year just for 1 prescription. Just think, if I was one of the people who had to take 2 to 3 or maybe even 4 pills a day I could not afford them out of pocket.

The Ryan White program is an available resource for anyone who has tested positive for HIV/AIDS but can't afford the medication. Ryan White was a teenager from Indiana who died of AIDS in 1990 because he could not afford the costly medication. The doctor or case manager will sign you up immediately but the decision is up to YOU to start taking the medication. If your count falls below 200 and you test positive for AIDS, they start you on the medication regardless, right then and there.

I have compassion for those people who signed up too late and have to be added to the waiting list. That list can take anywhere from 6 months to a year before you are covered. Some people don't make it that long and die because they decided to take the medication too late or can not get the medication due to financial barriers.

******

When I found out I started taking my medication right away. I was prescribed Atripla; this "Cocktail" has 3 other HIV pills in one tablet. Atripla is 1100 mg total combined with Sustiva, Emtriva and Viread. I would soon find out why they called the pill Atripla.

Once I started my medication in the beginning the side effects were severe. I felt like I was "TRIPPING" Seriously! The doctor had warned me beforehand about the possible side effects, but the side effects varies from person to person depending on a number of factors and how body weight and the immune system are important factors and she was not lying.

She told me the first time I take the pill, I will know that it's working by the way it will make me feel because it goes directly into your bloodstream if taken according to the directions.

The medication comes with very clear directions just like any other medication prescribed by a doctor. If taken correctly, your CD4+ will stay above 200, your viral load level will remain low and the virus will be undetectable. You will still have HIV but the virus in your body will be tremendously low.

The medication that I take is recommended at bedtime taken with a full glass of water and accommodated by at least 8 to 10 hours of sleep. Anything less than that you may feel the medication while it's working within your system. Consuming dairy or fatty foods within an hour before or after taking the medicine will double the possibility of adverse side effects.

The first time I took the drug that was prescribed to me I thought I was spinning in my sleep. I had all sorts of unimaginable nightmares. These nightmares were worse than any I'd ever had before. They were extremely frightening to the point that I didn't want to go to sleep at night let alone continue to take the pill ever again.

Once I had awaken that morning after taking the pill which was very early due to being extremely thirsty, the drug was still taking effect in my body. I could barely walk, I was not focused and keeping my balance required conscious effort and descending the stairs in my loft apartment was a major undertaking. When I returned to my room after getting a bottle of water from the refrigerator and the mountainous hike back up the stairs, I was exhausted. This was something that I sometimes experienced when I came home drunk from the club or a wild party. Drunk was exactly how I felt; like I had swam in a pool of alcohol.

When I saw my bed, I immediately began to cry. I hadn't realized I was wet and my bed was drenched; just as it was when I was having nightmares about gut wrenching events mentioned in "Eyes Without A Face." I hadn't urinated on myself while I was sleep either. I was having chronic "Night Sweats." My comforter, 2 of my 4 pillows were on the floor next to the bed and my sheets were off the mattress circled just like a tornado. The circle was the exact way that I felt while I was sleeping. I was indeed spinning around in my sleep. I stood there amazed and scared at the same time so I called my doctor.

She went through the regular routine questions and said most people experience the same side effects for the first couple of weeks.

Well I had become one of that "most people" for sure. She was right, after a couple of weeks, I had very little side effects; unless I had been drinking before I took the pill which is not a good thing so I don't make that a habit, only for special occasions.

Today, I am currently undetectable and my CD4+ is over 800. I have gained most of my weight back. I still have HIV but I feel good and look great.

CHAPTER 5

MY FAMILY & FRIEND'S REACTION TO MY STATUS

Naturally before I could even get out that I had HIV my mother told everyone for me. At the time that she told everyone, I wasn't even positive; my husband Price was. I needed someone to console me and I didn't want to say my husband had it so I told my mother that I had it. I know every child feels no matter what that when things go wrong they can call on their mother. A mother will always be there to make whatever situation right, well not my mother. She told the entire family and all of my friends before I knew it. Instead of saying I was HIV Positive, she said I was dying of AIDS.

******

I had finally come to grips with why my mother treated me the way she did. It was her coping skill being that she had a rough child, teen and young adult life. The cycle was coming back to her and she didn't know how to break it, so instead she continued it.

From the time my mother was born, something was wrong with her. As a baby, she broke out into a deep fever and her eyes rolled to the back of her head. My grandmother said ever since then she was a problem child only getting worse with time.

Her teenaged years were somewhat horrible because she loved to fight. Fight anyone that is, from her brothers, sisters, family members and she even stabbed a police officer in the back. The police officer was harassing my uncle Leon and my mom went crazy. She beat my aunt Sylvia as a child and teenager to the point where my aunt was actually afraid of my mother. She used to beat her with wire hangers. She also beat her oldest sister Denise. To this day, her relationship with my Aunt Denise is strained. No one trusts her because she is like day and night. One moment she is fine and the next she is telling you things that make you think that she is crazy.

She once called my great-grandmother and told her that her daughter, my grandmother had just died in a car accident. My grandmother had given my mother an ultimatum when she got pregnant with my sister. My mother was 14 years old and had just given birth to my brother. She had gone back for her 6 week checkup and was pregnant again. She had the option to abort my sister, give up my brother, give my sister up for adoption or move out.

So she gave my sister to her aunt who in return kept my sister from my mother. I know that had to be hard on my mother. After all, she had made the choice to have my sister and not give her up and then basically to have her taken away anyway was probably unbearable. Then she broke up with her first love which was the father of her two children. I could only imagine that pain.

I remember when my mother and dad Robert were in the process of breaking up and they had gotten in an argument in front of Pulaski Middle School which was where my dad worked. He must have put his hands in the car window and she rolled the window up and pulled off. We were in a gold 2 door Chevy Caprice and I was looking out the back window as I saw my dad passed out on the pavement in the middle of the street. I just cried out because my dad was just lying there unconscious in the street as we kept driving. She told me to shut the fuck up, turn around and sit down. I will never forget that. I was 7 years old and this was right after she had left my brother and me with my dad and moved to Texas.

You would think that the love between a mother and her children would be stronger than all the evil in the world which is definitely not the case with my mother and her children. My sister and I relationships are strained with our mother. My sister has 2 children, one of which my mother has met and the other she's yet to meet.

******

Returning for the 2nd time to Minnesota after moving from there in April of 2010 to Dallas, Texas and while at my grandmother Hazel's 75th Birthday party, I decided then was the perfect time for me to come out to my family. I told my girl cousins first, I did this in two separate groups starting with the older girls, then I told my nieces and Rachel.

Watching them all cry I knew it was going to be even harder to break the news to my brother. The way that they all cried made me feel sorry for the person with the disease. I had to remember that it was me that was living with HIV because I had totally forgotten that it was me. I got so wrapped up into everyone's tears that I almost thought it was someone else's that we were talking about.

My sister already knew because I told her right away after I found out. We kept nothing from each other but it was my mother's comfort that I was seeking when I said my husband had it. My brother was in total disbelief and told me to quit lying. I had to pull him outside of the party to let him know I wasn't joking.

All I wanted at that time was his love and support, and my brother gave me just that. He hugged me and kissed my head for the first time in his life and said the words that I had been longing to hear, "I love you man and you're going to be okay, I am here for you with whatever you need, you're my little brother." I could have broken down right then and there but I had to remain strong; I was at my grandmother's birthday party and I didn't want everyone to be sad because of the news that I had just delivered. This was supposed to be a special occasion, my grandmother had just turned 75 years old!

Believe it or not, I think my status made my brother and my relationship stronger and even closer or it may have been the actions that took place after the reading of "Eyes Without A Face." My brother almost went crazy finding out his friends had, had sex with me so he wanted to kill them. Romie and some of his friends from Minnesota had driven to Gary only 2 days after I had the book reading in Minnesota and I had to beg him to let it go and not do anything stupid. I told him it was the past and I had let it go. Plus I've let the world know by putting it in my book. To this day, my brother calls me so much that I can honestly say it's a bit much at times; but I love it.

I then told my grandmother, and to my surprise, she just hugged me and told me she loved me for me and that I was still her grandson regardless of what I had and everything was going to be alright, just watch. I then realized why grandma did what she did in my past and after speaking with her she confirmed it. She had no knowledge of openly gay people then and didn't know how to accept it. She only went by what she knew and what she saw from everyone else. I also understood why she did for my other cousins and not for my brother and me. My grandmother said that she did for those that did not have a father as she saw many men in and out of our lives. That was so true but half true, the men she saw wasn't there for my brother and me, they were there for my mother.

Letting my mother's side of the family know about my HIV status was the easiest thing that I had ever done. Being forced out gay was harder than that. I had to think in the back of my mind, "Did they think I was going to catch HIV anyway?" After I told my immediate family, I had no problem telling my other cousins, aunts, uncles and extended family. I didn't care so much that I cared about them.

I didn't want them to have to go through what I had been going through by holding it in, taking my meds every night or even going to the clinic to give blood every three months. I felt degraded going to give blood to monitor my T Cell closely so I learned more about the disease because I had it. I was intrigued and I wanted to help others after finding out about my own health.

******

Now telling my father's side of the family was hard for me. I was still getting to know some and didn't want to really tell the ones that I knew in fear of rejection or judgment, but I had to tell someone. I haven't quite told everyone as of yet although after they read this book they will know.

I decided to tell the ones closest to me with time, aunts Ann and Mary were of the first to know. I was nervous and I was just telling them of my daily routine and me visiting the clinics here in Atlanta and speaking to other HIV Positive people that had just learned of their status when I realized mid-way through our conversation that I had spilled the tea.

Neither one said anything while we were on the phone, but my Aunt Ann called right back after we all hung up and said the words that linger with me today. "Baby, I heard what you said, I just want you to know that if you ever want to talk or need anything your Aunt is just a phone call away. Please don't ever hesitate and I love you so much. OKAY?"

I was shocked but not shocked. Aunt Ann was always supportive from the first day I met her. That made me call Aunt Mary back to tell her because I felt the same exact way about her as I did Aunt Ann. I loved them like I'd known them all my life. In fact, I looked at them like my Aunts Sylvia and Teresa. They always made me feel special.

After I gathered my thoughts a few hours later I called Aunt Mary back. When she answered the phone, it sounded like she was expecting me to call back. We started talking about the gay clubs and what made me gay. She was very intrigued and at the end of the conversation, Aunt Mary said, "I can call her whenever and never not go without calling her for a long period of time or she would be on her way to Atlanta to check up on me."

Then she said, "I just want you to know I will always love and support you. You are my brother's son, my nephew and I will always be here." She said I love you and I will speak to you later and we hung up. That conversation had me in tears. She was sincere how she said it and I just thanked GOD because I was just about half way through the hard part.

I decided to tell my cousins Marcellus, Tori, Demetri, Marcus and Vickie because I felt very close to them. I felt that I shouldn't have any secrets from them and I just wanted to be open and honest. Why should I have to feel ashamed of something I have I thought. Either they would support me or they would walk away from me. At this point in my life, either way was fine with me with some people.

My cousin Tori which is my Aunt Ann's daughter was first because she was the only girl that I was close to and I knew she would support me off top. I just knew in return that it would hurt her feelings. I called her on the phone after she got out of school. We always talked so this was nothing new. I asked how her day was going and everything then just said, "Look, I have something to tell you!" She said okay, "What?"

"I have HIV!" Tori reply was very simple, "Okay, just take care of yourself boy." WOW, that went to good and we carried on our conversation before hanging up, but before we hung up, she said, "You know you don't have to tell everyone until you're ready and just be careful and remember to tell your partner." I already knew that but I said ok and we said our goodbyes.

On my way to Alabama for Easter with my cousin Demetri who is Tori little's brother and his girlfriend Nalaysha, we all were speaking about my book and in general. Lots of topics were brought up. When the topic of HIV came up, I got nervous. I thought for a second that maybe Tori had told Demetri but the thought went away.

So I just went and said what I was doing as far as visiting clinics in Georgia, speaking to new patients that tested Positive for HIV and AIDS. I said that, that was my passion now, and I knew they both caught on because the car got silent for a couple seconds afterwards and Demetri just bursted out and said, "But you do know that it's not a death sentence now right?" I said of course and we started speaking about the medications and all that. I didn't have to come right out and say it but I knew that they knew after that.

My cousin Marcellus had come to his son's gradation here in Georgia from Memphis with girlfriend Yolanda. We were out drinking at a bar & grill in midtown Atlanta and just like that, out of nowhere, I just started speaking of the clinics and what I was doing there. I think that was my comfort zone. I was doing something to help someone else and if saving someone by telling them what I had and what I was trying to do to prevent others from getting what I had then I had to say it.

Marcellus and his girlfriend's response were all the same. It was like everyone already knew or just had some knowledge already about the disease.

My cousin Marcus is Marcellus' little brother and we attended Kennedy King Middle School together back in the day. We were at Cousin Vickie's house in July during Vickie son's graduation party when I told him and Cousin Vickie but at separate times. We were eating our Barbecue at the table outside when I said it. He had nothing to say but, "It's okay cuz, you'll be okay man." That went super great and quick.

It was on to Vickie right after that. I was just making my way through the family without any hesitation or regret. Vickie is my cousin Marcellus' baby mother. They had the twins together and she was also my karaoke partner.

She took it just like I thought she would while I told her as we were speaking to each other outside in our own little world. She told me I would be okay and if I needed anything, she was just a phone call away or a quick 15 minute trip from my house, she was so warming.

******

Telling my friends was the easiest thing that I'd ever done in my entire life. Angela, Michial, Lester, Michelle, Molly, Tyeastia, Damien, Avern, and so many others were super supportive. I could not have asked for a better support system however, I did lose some real close family members and friends in the process but hey, it was their lost and not mine. I didn't have anything to loose so I really didn't care. I had major people in my life to support me and that's all that really mattered. Everyone else can kick rocks with sandals on.

A lot of us that are HIV Positive go through our own stage when we feel that it's time to tell our family and friends. As for me, my time was quick and some I had to tell because they were told a lie from my mother and others. I told because I wanted to and the rest was because I was trying to protect them from catching it. I wanted to let them know that this disease was now at their backdoor and none of them were exempt from it.

CHAPTER 6

MY MARRIAGE & MY EX

With all the signs I saw that Price showed me I didn't want to see them. It took me even longer to see why he did the things he did. It didn't hit me until one day I was thinking of what was it that he stated that he actually wanted in his mate. He said things to me that would make sense as to what he was looking for and why.

He told me that he wanted his dick to be as big as his father's. He said that he and his father would take baths together when he was a child. He said some days his dad would come into the bathroom when he was naked brushing his teeth and would urinate, but he would also be naked. Price stated that his dad would approach him from behind and hold him. One day, Price showed me exactly how his dad would hold him. His penis would rest on Price ass. Did Price father molest him and had he not said anything? That question would never be answered.

******

What a mess Price had created and he didn't even know it. My cycle was beginning as his cycle was ending. I didn't want a relationship, nor did I trust anyone and everyone was out to get something from me, I was jaded and bitter. I believed all men were dogs. It took me a while to come back that every man wasn't like Price.

DL Men had stability and I was in Atlanta and that's what I wanted. I knew I could have it because I had what it took to turn a man that I wanted the way I wanted them to be. I'm not saying every man will turn but honestly, I've only had 1 in my day that didn't, and you know what they say, "Once you go gay you stay that way."

I still and always will love Price with all my heart. He was the first of many things in my life that I will carry with me until the day I die. He was the first gay man that I had ever slept with, my first boyfriend, my first love, first person that I was ever with for so long and my first marriage that I thought would never happen. He was the first guy that I ever had sex with that was "Trish" in other words he was Trade and Fish is what we called men like him in Gay Terms. As I have stated in "Eyes Without A Face" I did a lot of things to keep him when he didn't want to be kept.

I sold my soul to the devil to have someone that didn't want me. He used me in every way that he could, he didn't put a gun to my head or anything I did it because I wanted to. I did it because I loved him and I thought he loved me; I was looking for love in all the wrong places.

I relegated myself to living a life that was mostly unhappy with him; I degraded myself to the fullest. I did things that I was not proud of but I knew it would make him happy and as long as he happy so was I.

Price was very freaky and nasty, I'd only seen one side of him though, however Lucciano experienced the other side and after hearing his stories I'm glad it was him and not me. The shit stains explained it all, he was an uninhibited freak. That explained further why he would get upset or blow things out of proportion if I wanted to shower before sex, he liked it nasty. In fact, Lucciano said Price loved for him to shit on his dick. This happened just about every time when they were together during their short three month on and off again span. I told Price of course what Lucciano told me and he said it only happened by mistake. **Side Stare**

******

While I was at the hospital in West Virginia visiting Lucciano, we shared our life stories from beginning to end. We talked until he fell asleep every night. We talked about how much we had in common and the things we didn't, unlike myself, his family was very open and supportive to him being gay. We talked about our health and our CD4+ count. He taught me some things about HIV that I didn't know and his doctor taught me more. My friendship with Lucciano grew even closer after the hospital visit where we talked about everything and I do mean everything. I even explained to Lucciano how to use an enema to ensure that he wouldn't leave a Picasso painting.

We had to lie to his doctor and nurses about us being brothers in order to get all the information that they wanted him to know. He couldn't take any more bad news and I was there to deliver it in a positive manner. We laughed and cried together. We bond within those seven days while staying there with him. This would be the first time that we ever hung together without Price. I had only seen Lucciano twice in my life before going to West Virginia. Those two times included me driving to Chicago; once to fight him and the other for Price's mom and my birthday party which we had celebrated together the year before in December of 2009.

Eventually we talked about Price and why they split up in the first place. I think he loved Price more than I did. He told me what he did to push Price's buttons which led to huge arguments. He also told me the things he and Price did to build their bond. Price loved men that were hard core and said, "No" to him sometimes. I was a "Yes" guy to Price's dominance. I always said yes, I couldn't say no to him.

We listened to music on my laptop in the room and I showed him the beginning chapters of *"Eyes Without A Face."* We compared friends on Facebook, looked at cute boys and of course discussed the boys we'd slept with. He showed me his family members and I showed him mine, it was good to put faces to the names that we'd shared.

******

While in his hospital room that next morning, it was very sunny outside. I would say it had to be around 80 degrees there, but it felt nice. The birds were chirping and the nurses were delivering breakfast to all the hospital residents. They had even brought me a tray. But everyone knows my cycle; something good is always followed by something bad. The devil had crept back into my life faster than a speeding bullet. My husband was calling Lucciano while we enjoyed breakfast.

They talked for a few minutes and he was being "Mr. Nice Guy" to Lucciano. I called that bastard Price while I was boarding the plane in Cali to let him know why I was going to West Virginia and I told him to call Lucciano to express his feelings because it could be the last time they spoke. He told me, "Fuck you and fuck Lucciano!" He didn't care about either one of us. I told him that it wasn't that serious, and I didn't want to argue at that time. I just needed him to support his ex before I hung up on his ignorant ass.

Lucciano had Price on speaker phone and I heard Price say, "I don't have any money to come visit, Sam should have bought me a plane ticket being that he has all the money and left me with none!" When in reality, Price had already committed identity theft against me stealing more than $25,000.00 in a combination of cash advances, credit card fraud and bills! Price was saying to Lucciano how sorry he was about his health, and how Lucciano should have told him about it. He stated that Lucciano could always come talk to him! Price also stated, "No matter what happens between us you should always be able to come to me." This was Price's signature line that he told everybody!!!

He asked, "Where's my husband?" Lucciano said, "Right here!" Then he asked to speak with me. Once I answered the phone, **Like I wasn't already sitting next to the phone on speaker** Price began to curse me out! Once again, I was every stupid, ignorant, dumb bitch in his book! He stated that he couldn't stand me, and that I was going to pay for leaving him high and dry in Dallas, Texas. I laughed and said, "Fuck you, you dumb broke ass bitch!" Price then stated, "You think I'm broke?!"

By the end of that day the power company had turned off the lights at our house and Price was upset at both of us when he called back. He told Lucciano, "Don't worry; you're going to die before me, and don't fucking text or call me no damn more!"

******

It was right there, in that room, at that very moment when I asked Lucciano if I could add him to my book. I felt that he had earned a place in my book. Without any hesitation he said, "Yes I'm all for it." We wanted to show people how two ex's can become best of friends in a time of need. We even posted on each other's Facebook page, "I am friends with my ex's ex. Is this possible?" And of course we had so many comments; both good and bad. Like I stated before, that could have been Price or myself lying in that hospital room and I knew in my heart I would have wanted someone there with me.

I was there to encourage Lucciano when he thought he wouldn't be here on earth anymore. When the doctors delivered the news that he may not walk out, I was there to let him know that he would. I was there to make things right even when the doctors would come in to deliver bad news as well as when the nurses were taking blood and couldn't find a vein due to dehydration. I was there to tell the nurse to take it from the other arm which was painful because she stuck him in the wrong place. I would even massage his aching body until he'd eventually fall asleep.

It wasn't his time yet and my sister would call or I would call her and we'd pray daily to assure that he knew that. Although I had no clue what I was actually reading, I knew that GOD led me in the scriptures I read. If GOD did call him home, he was not going to be alone. I was going to be right there next to him holding his hand. I loved him like he was my little brother. We shared the same birthday, December 15th so other than being my ex's ex, we shared something else incredible.

I will never forget the day that Lucciano was able to walk on his own. I gave him my clothes and we strolled our asses down to the cafeteria disregarding his doctor's orders not to leave the room. Lucciano wanted to get out and I wanted to make sure he was happy so we did. Mother's Day was approaching and I wanted to get my sister and mother-in-law something before I left because I knew I was leaving that Sunday which was Mother's Day and I wouldn't have time to do that once I was back in Cali.

After visiting the hospital's gift store, we decided that I should mail my mother in law gift right away and the Post Office was only across the street so that's what we did. We headed right out the front door to the Post Office to mail her gift. We took a chance but like I said, if he was going to die, I wanted to ensure that he would be happy and get to do everything he wanted to do even if it was just the littlest thing.

The next day Lucciano called his friend who lived in West Virginia because he was craving Popeye's chicken and his to take him. While his friend was there with us in the hospital room, we told him that Lucciano had problems with his lungs do to smoking and he knew he wasn't supposed to be smoking. **Side Stare** Lucciano will be released soon is what we told his friend so he wouldn't ask too many questions. This was the day I was returning to Cali. We ordered our chicken and ate right there at Popeye's and I tell you, that was the best chicken I've ever eaten in my life, I still can taste it today. After we were done, we all returned to his hospital room like we never left. I packed my bags and his great aunt was already in route to take me back to the airport.

Once his great aunt and uncle arrived, Lucciano and his friend walked me down to the front entrance of the hospital where we said our goodbyes. This was the first time that I didn't want to let him go and it seemed like we hugged forever telling each other we loved one another. Finally, I was off to the airport headed back to what I was now calling my new home; Cali.

******

After Price and I broke up the first time and got back together, Price told me that he wanted a three way relationship, I wanted to please him desperately so I reluctantly agreed to it. It started with us having threesomes; mind you, we were not married nor had we even thought of getting married at that point in our relationship. The threesomes eventually lead us to being involved in a three way relationship, this is how it all went down.

Our first threesome was with a guy I knew that worked at the gas station up the street from our house. His name was Thomas and he was straight; supposedly. He was red boned about 6'2", 180 pounds solid with hazel eyes. He was everything I wanted plus he was straight. I made the call to Thomas informing him on what was about to go down. He was drunk and horny so he was mad game. We picked him up and brought him back to the house. Once we arrived, Price turned on a flick and we both started kissing each other after we all got undressed. Thomas laid on the bed too drunk to stand up. Price started kissing Thomas like there was no tomorrow. I felt my anger building and I got pissed but I kept giving both of them head.

After a while, Thomas couldn't maintain an erection and Price got irritated. Price lost interest and decided that we could get off by ourselves so we took Thomas home. "Fuck!" Our first threesome didn't work and I really wanted to have sex with Thomas that night. However when we returned home Price exceeded all of my expectations. That night Price had found a new drive, filled with an unbelievably, animalistic passion which made my heart race and body heave with uncontrollable desire. For the first time since our first time together Price seemed to be passionately in love with me.

His touch was electrifying as his hands caressed my body and his kiss took my breath away and I hoped it would never end. That wasn't the case for Price though.

The following weekend, Price bought some Ecstasy and we both popped a pill. It was a Saturday night and we were going to the Gay 90s Club. This was my first time popping Ecstasy. He told me about the way the pill will make us feel but the feeling was nothing like he described. He said we would be mad horny. I don't even know the words to explain how horny I was. I was ready for anything as long as I was doing it with Price.

Price laid out his plan; we were to hunt for a versatile guy, someone Price could fuck while they're fucking me. He said we were only choosing the finest of dudes to bring home. Upon our arrival the hunt was on as we went our separate ways seeking the perfect prey. I was looking for a redbone who was masculine and I was pleased when I came across someone I'd encountered sexually in my past. I knew he was versatile back then but he had a child; that's why we didn't go any further. His name was Dawayne, he was a redbone, 5'10", 150 pounds, slender build and was willing to do anything.

Price and I took him back to our house where we were all tipsy, Price and I were rolling off Ecstasy and Dawayne was rolling off whatever. It was truly a freak session in the beginning as we all began kissing each other. Next thing I knew Price was on his back and I was on top riding him while Dawayne's face was deep in Price's ass tossing his salad {Eating ass} Then Price wanted Dawayne to fuck me. I was ready but Dawayne couldn't get hard, he had turned into a strict bottom by this time and I didn't even know. So Price threw Dawayne's legs up and began to fuck him.

In the beginning while Price was fucking him, I started eating Price's ass. This was my first time I'd ever done this to him but he was my man and I wanted to make sure I pleased him and I'd saw that he liked what Dawayne was doing. This was the first time I'd ever seen Price's asshole and I was turned off. There was some kind of ball or knot hanging out of Price's ass and to make matters worse, he was fucking the shit out of Dawayne by this time. I got jealously pissed and just laid back and watched try to jack my now soft dick. I wanted to make sure that he was happy but I wasn't. As Price came, he let out the loudest moan that I had ever heard him make. I was jealous as hell. This bitch Dawayne just gave my man the best nut ever.

On the way taking Dawayne home, neither Price nor I said a word to each other. Price knew I was mad. After Dawayne got out the car, I began to cry, my feelings were crushed. Price told me then that it was just sex and he knew where home was and would never leave me for anyone. I stopped crying but my feelings were still hurt.

We slowed down on the threesomes for about a month until Price brought it back up again. I insisted that we go with what he wanted in the first place; a three way relationship verses doing random threesomes. He agreed, but this time I wanted someone from out of state. That's where Gary came into play.

Gary was someone that I had met and turned out the first time Price and I broke up. I had gone to Orlando to start over because I couldn't live in Minnesota knowing that Price was fucking everyone around me. Gary was straight and had a girlfriend but that was quickly over after the first time we hooked up. I had turned him out and he wanted me no matter what.

I told Gary that I was back in my relationship with Price. He didn't care as long as he could have me. I told him about the three way relationship idea and he was down, so he flew from Florida and came to Minnesota. Gary was dark skin, 6'0, 190 pounds, with a 13 inch shoe. He was a pretty chocolate boy and I wasn't really attracted to chocolate men. Instantly I fell for him from the first time I saw him and I knew Price would too, he was so damn manly.

Once Gary arrived in Minnesota, they had differences right off the bat. Gary felt that he should do everything for me like open the car door, any other door, pay for everything and rub my feet too once I got off work. This is what I had done for Price. I never opened doors for Price but I was constantly rubbing his feet like he had worked a nine to five. I did it because I loved him.

Price didn't like the attention that Gary was giving me, but Gary was willing to do anything keep me. Even if that meant that he would let Price fuck him, he would as long as I allowed him to be with us.

The first and last time we all tried to have sex was a disaster. Price started it off with tossing my salad. Then while I started giving Price head, Gary started tossing my salad. Price then started fucking me, and I mean he fucked me so good. There was definitely a difference in Price's stroke. He was in competition with someone who was in love with me and someone who had a bigger dick. I was in heaven. Then Price tried to fuck Gary. No luck there because Gary shitted on Price dick and he wanted to stop but of course Price didn't want too. After Gary and Price cleaned up, Gary came back and started fucking me.

This would be the first time that I ever saw Price get jealous because someone else was doing a better job than him, he left the room and never came back. The next day, Price gave me an ultimatum. Either Gary goes back to Florida or Price was going back to Chicago. Of course you know what happened, Gary went back to Florida. While taking Gary to the airport, he told me how much he loved me and he knew that he wasn't going to be allowed to come back. He said he would do anything to keep me or even keep us.

Hell, in the short time that I knew Gary, he had paid my rent, bought Price and I, new cell phones so we all could have chirp and even put money in our pockets but I was in love with Price and not him so I told him to be easy. That was the first time I had ever had a guy cry over me as I had cried over Price when we first broke up. Gary told me as he exited the car to check in at the airport, "He is going to break your damn heart and you are going to look like a damn fool in the end." Who the hell was he kidding? I was not giving up Price for him even if I was taking care of Price and he didn't have a pot to piss in or a window to throw it out of. I didn't love him, I loved Price.

******

Three months later I left California and returned to Dallas, after Price and I broke up, I still wanted him. I felt like I knew Price better than I had known myself. While I was in California, Price informed me that he was invited to do a threesome with two other guys. Although he said he didn't do it I'd begged to differ because it was not like Price to pass up an opportunity like that.

When I returned I tried to figure out what needed to be done so I could keep Price. I was willing to do anything to have him by my side. I got on BGC {Black Gay Chat or the Boys and Girls Club} again. This was the same site that initially broke us up in the beginning. I was on a mission now looking for strict bottoms or versatile bottoms that wouldn't mind indulging in a threesome with the both of us. While I was looking for someone on BGC, someone else was hitting me up too.

This dude who had a white roommate wanted me to do a three-some with he and his friend. He assumed that I was a top from my profile picture. We chatted for a bit before exchanging phone numbers. After our conversation, I learned that they both were bottoms looking to get fucked. Anything goes is what the boy told me after he gave me his address and phone number. I'd told him about Price but I said that we were best friends instead of him being my husband or boyfriend.

Once Price came back home from one of his rendezvous, I told him what I had conjured up. His face lit up when I told him it was two bottoms looking for anything as long as we were tops. On the way there, Price made sure that this was something that I wanted to do not just him; either way he was down for it. I was willing to do anything at that point. Hell I knew I was degrading myself but what did I have left to lose, I'd already lost my husband.

We knocked on the door and the boys let us in. They had liquor and weed, I felt like I was getting primed for one of my escorting gigs. I knew I had to perform my best to capture my husband's attention. While we were smoking and drinking I had to endure these two boys complementing my husband and me on how good we looked. They wanted to make sure that we were cool with switching off after we got going. They wanted us both to fuck both of them. I felt myself getting extremely nervous as I knew it was about to go down. Then one of the boys insisted that we be in separate rooms. Price went with the black boy first and I went with the white boy.

Once we were in the room, the boy began to give me head. I couldn't even get hard because I was too busy thinking of what

Price and the other boy were doing in the other room. Within minutes, there was a knock at the door. Price wanted all of us to be in the same bed so we could watch each other fuck. I was nervous as hell being that I had never done this before {Me being the top in front of Price}. Price put on a condom while the black boy laid face down on the bed with his legs spread wide opened. The white boy stood over his black friend and began to receive head from him. I was supposed to go behind the white boy and start fucking him as Price was fucking the black boy. Once again; I couldn't even get an erection.

I then began to think to myself, was this really worth keeping someone that didn't want to be kept. Furthermore, I knew in my heart that this, having threesomes or foursomes would never stop. This is what turned Price on. After a while Price had fucked both boys while I just stood there and watched trying to get hard playing with myself. Finally, Price took notice of me and got pissed off. He just pulled his dick out the white boy's ass, took off the condom and started putting his clothes on. The others kept going, sucking each other as we were getting dressed. I could see the madness in Price's face. He really wanted to do this and I had just fucked it all up.

The entire ride home, he cursed me out and called me every dumb stupid ass bitch in the book. He insisted "I don't ever want you to bring this shit up again. You set the shit up and you couldn't even get hard. I was right there in your face so I thought I would be an extra added incentive for you to get hard being that you want me so badly." All I could do was cry.

*****

In March of 2011 after being in Atlanta, Georgia for almost three months, I knew my relationship was indeed over. It was over after I left Dallas the first time but I knew for sure it was over in March. I felt no love for Price in the way that a man is supposed to love someone of that nature. I thought over and over and over and again how he left me in the hospital and alone once I was released. We were finished.

To clear my memories of being married, Avern took me to a local pawn shop so I could pawn the wedding band. I thought that it would be easy but the jeweler offered me $60.00 for a $2,200.00, 1 Karat princess cut white gold band. I was heated and as we looked around so I could have time to make my mind up, I overheard the jeweler trying to sell a wedding band to a woman. She didn't have much money and was really trying to buy a specific type of band that was similar to mine.

I walked over and introduced myself to her and asked how long had she and her fiancé been together. She replied, "Five years" and they were ready for the next step. She said that they had been through marriage counseling at their church and was given the green light to get married but hard times fell on them and she really couldn't afford a good band. She said something that I will never forget, "At the end of the day, it's just my husband and me and I can't go broke trying to buy a band." I replied, "That's exactly what my husband used to say to me." I told her that we used the term, "You and Me."

The look on her face left me almost in tears. She said that's she and her fiancé all day. I then told her what I had inscribed inside of my wedding band which was, "You and Me." I asked her what size did he wear and she said the magic word, he was a size seven; so was I. I immediately took the band off and told her to give it to her husband. The band deserved to be on someone's finger who would give the same love in return.

She offered me $200.00 for my band. GOD was on her side that day, I turned down the money and I told her to cherish it forever. I wanted to cherish it as well but it no longer had the same meaning to me. It was just a piece of jewelry to me now, plus Price had pawned his that July in Dallas and just like that, we walked out the pawn shop with no money and I had no wedding band. I felt good inside because I knew someone with love for the person they were with were going to be now representing "You and Me."

******

Price and I have been separated now for over two years. As much as I did want him, I didn't anymore. When I look back and see how I degraded myself and how I allowed him to treat me, disgusted me. I hated myself for even allowing anyone to have that much control over me. Price had taken all of my energy and it has taken up until this point to restore.

As far as a divorce, it was going to be hard to get one. I called California to seek a divorce and was told that one of us would have to be a resident there for six months. Hell no, I wasn't moving back to California. I missed my sister, nieces, brother in law and friends but there was no way I was making that trip down the road again. I had all my furniture this time and I was not about to do that.

Subsequently I sought a divorce lawyer here in Atlanta and I was told no by all except one lawyer who stated, "Gay Marriage is not recognized in the state of Georgia that we would have to go through the Supreme Court" and I was ready for that. The only thing was that it cost and it wasn't by far cheap. It would be $3,700.00 just to retain him, $250.00 an hour and $350.00 for court filing fees. I wasn't rich nor was I in the mood to sell my body again so getting a divorce was now on the back burner.

This was around tax season and my Cousin Felicia's best friend Delores was trying to contact me. Price had taken Delores' cousin's children's information and filed them. I eventually called Price and asked him if he had filed the kids and to my surprise he did not deny it. He said he had to live and he needed the money. I asked how much did he get back and he told me over $5,000.00. I asked him if he would go half with me for the divorce so we both could be free. He told me plain and simple, "Hell No, we haven't been together in a year come next month so we are divorced in my eyes." I was speechless.

CHAPTER 7

SOME GAY MEN CAN'T BE FAITHFUL

Just because you're gay doesn't mean you have to lust over every boy you see. You don't have to be loud and or flamboyant. Just be yourself without all of the extra's. Being flamboyant is how we end up being judged, ridiculed and hurt by others. We have to remember that people won't judge what they can't see.

I've learned that some gay men can't be faithful because they have some insecurity problems within themselves so to release their frustration and pain many gay men engage in worthless sex. I felt this way long before being in a relationship and I know what I am talking about. Sometimes we gay men have sex based on the fact that we have low self-esteem; we know that we are too fine so we just do it to be doing it. Sometimes out of anger or simply a scheme to manipulate others for materialistic gain, things that they can buy themselves by simply getting a job. I had a job but I had a shopping habit; I had to have everything that I never had and in return I did all types of things to get it.

I was satisfying my need for intimacy and killing my insecurities all at the same time I thought. I was either fucking or cuddling and it was just the need of being with someone different all the time. I didn't build feelings for a long time; I simply shut down. I would think of how my mother or brother would beat me, I would think of the fact that they never held or hugged me, never genuinely said I love you when I was younger. I often conjured those thoughts in my mind often while having casual sex.

Gay men just love stealing other men that are already in relationships then they go bragging about how they stole that person. They feel that they can have them so they go after what they want until they get it. Typically they even cause a breakup and end up with the guy in most situations only to find that they never wanted the person but rather to satisfy a self-fulfilling sickness. The one thing they fail to realize is how you get him is exactly how you lose him. Women are like that too but the gay man takes the cake on this one. I was guilty by association.

Some gay men are just so visual. Everything that looks good, they have to have. Most of us in our community are prejudice and don't even know it. We go after the men that are buff with muscles, pretty face and nice in the waist. They can come with nothing and yet we still don't care, as long as they look good and the dick is great we will take their ass in.

I was just like that. I never wanted to really fall in love, I just wanted someone fine and great in bed. I didn't want to get hurt nor did I want to hurt anyone else.

Adonis was the first person that I really had feelings for. He was different than the average fine DL man, he actually came with something; a career, a bank account with money in it. He was still collecting a check from the Army.

Adonis and another straight guy other than Price were the men that I had been with for long periods of time. Adonis and I lasted exactly 9 months, he was beyond fine. His name fit him just perfect and he was perfect in every way. The only problem was that Adonis was engaged. He was actually someone else man and it's not even like I didn't know. I knew going in and I felt in my heart that I could have him completely.

When it was my time to have him completely after his fiancée found out from their 5 year old son, I didn't want it anymore. All I could think of was how he did her with me and that he was definitely going to do the same to me. I didn't want to get hurt because I started to have feelings for him and I seen where that was going before we even went there so I had to let that go and neither one of us got hurt in that process.

Karma had a different plan because I didn't get anything negative back from him. Instead after I was married my husband did the same exact thing to me that I had done to Adonis' fiancée. It took me a while to finally come to terms and accept that. But hey, "You reap what you sow" or what goes around comes right back around.

I learned later on in life after speaking with Adonis after *Eyes Without A Face* came out that he has another problem; he was a sex addict. Adonis said that he had to have sex like 5 to 6 times a day, well bust a nut to say the least. He told me that I was perfect because I would allow him to have me any way that he wanted. His insecurity was that he was too fine and he said he knew he could have anybody. Sometimes people feel that, that's an insecurity because people only use them for their good looks. What he didn't know and what I never told him was that I thought I was too fine too and I wanted him to have me in anyway there was. I wanted him probably just as bad as he wanted me.

******

It took me a long time to have self-control over my insecurities and the feeling of wanting to have sex to make it go away. I knew exactly what my insecurities were and I knew now how to fix them. I also knew what I wanted and what I had been through in my past after dealing with Price.

Price had many insecurities and right after we married they started to come out. Seeing his insecurities made me take action of my own. I knew he had some before we were married but I looked past them and tried to bring them to his attention. One was he thought that his dick was too little but it was just right for me. Just like what I had always known from gay men, he was so caught up in his looks that he felt like he should always have sex with someone new. He felt like he could never be alone. He wanted to have control over any and every thing.

He felt that he didn't have enough control over me in the beginning and he used to say that by him being my husband now that I should submit to him. He felt like the only thing he had control over was Tabby (the cat) and the front door. He made that very aware when Lisa, Felicia's best friend came over and Price nearly knocked her down because she knocked on our door verses ringing the doorbell.

Price and Lisa had started hanging real hard. They were going places and doing everything together. She was actually the first person to tell me that Price was cheating on me and that he was a girl. Of course I didn't believe her. They weren't even mad at each other at the time when she told me but she said being that she had known me for over 10 years that we were family and she had to say something, but her warnings had fallen on deaf ears.

Lisa had come over one day while we were living in Richfield along with Shamanda, Delores cousin and Janae. They were all coming over to get high as usual. I was off work this day and it was hot as hell. It was well over 100 degrees to be exact. Price had taped a note under the doorbell that read, "Ring doorbell do not knock" which was about a centimeter long.

Price went to the door in a rage and when he opened it, Lisa was making her way inside the house because of the heat. She had just called and said her air conditioner was out in her car, so have the door open. I don't know what the hell was wrong with Price but he grabbed and pushed her so hard that she flew back and almost hit her head on the brick wall. I'm glad Shamanda was there to catch her because if not, Lisa sure enough would have been fucked up.

Her arm was bruised and swollen from the fall. She is bi-racial (black and white) and very light skinned so her bruise showed clearly right away. She was crying and asking Price at first what the hell was wrong with him. She yelled and said she had just called, "I know you mad cos I knocked and didn't ring the doorbell, but damn nicca, it's hot as fuck out here! How could you do this to me?"

The neighbors saw what happened and told her they were calling the police, because he had just assaulted her. Lisa insisted that they don't and that she was just going to leave, all the while I kept trying to pull Price into the house to break them apart. This nicca was actually trying to fight her and would not back down. He called her all types bitches, in return out of anger she called him a "Punk ass broke faggot, who just mad cos the only thing that he has control over was Tabby and the fucking door.

She had known without me saying it so that meant that his insecurities were showing. Price was furious and saying that I was taking her side because I wouldn't let him out the door. I just kept telling him that she is a woman and he being a man; let it go! He actually wanted to fight her but I was not going to allow that to happen.

******

I knew for sure that hurt people hurt people because I was still hurting in a way over Price. So I hurt #26 because he was the closest person to me. #26 Saw a person who simply wanted to be loved. I saw someone who wanted someone to love them, and do right by them. At that time last year, I was not that person for him. I had been hurt so much, that I felt in my heart, that it was just a matter of time before he hurt me. So I did what any hurt person would do, I hurt him first, time after time and again.

I cheated and told him, but he stayed with me anyway; I was so lost. Although he cried in my arms I was still lost as to why would he stay with someone who had done him so wrong, but I felt his heart and understood his pain. It was the last week of May, 2012, I was out having drinks with my friends Demond and TK at the Daiquiri Factory. I just jumped up and said, I need to call my guy because something isn't right.

I called him and said, "Please call your mom!" Their relationship was like that of my ex Price, and his mother that I wanted with my own mother. He asked me why, and I said, please just call. He called, and called me back, and said everything was okay. The next morning, he called me crying hysterically. His mother had died later that night of a heart attack. We cried together for the next couple of days before he left to go back home to NYC. After he returned, I still had an uneasy feeling.

I had started to tell him that he needed to move back home to be with his family, being that he had none here in ATL. He thought it was because I was doing my dirt. Honestly, I was but I still felt some sort of way. The very next day, his grandmother, his mother's mom, passed away. They both died a week and a couple of days apart from one another, it hadn't even been a full two weeks.

He was a wreck and so was I, I felt his pain. I felt even more hurt because I was adding insult to injury by cheating. He was grieving the loss of his mother, and grandmother and there I was causing more pain by cheating.

Finally, August 4, 2012, he moved back to NYC which was the exact day that I was married to Price exactly four years earlier. I only realized after he was gone, that hurt people hurt people. People are brought into our lives for a reason, a season, and a lifetime. He was brought to me for a reason, just because I was hurt, didn't mean I had to hurt someone else in return. Everyone was not out to hurt me. I had to learn the hard way after seeing him leave. Unfortunately, I never got the chance to apologize for the pain I caused.

I'M SORRY BABY....I AM SO SORRY FROM THE BOTTOM OF MY HEART...FROM THE CORE OF MY SOUL...I LOVE YOU #26

******

Now having realized my own insecurities, I am not about to allow my past mistakes to hinder my present nor my future. I used all those mistakes as lessons and used them as stepping stones to know what to look out for and what to avoid, but that left me to deal with reconciling my sexuality with my spirituality.

First off I want to say, my body can't help what my flesh craves so I command my flesh to die daily. I fight with myself a lot because of my sexuality. Some days I feel like I should be straight and other days I just want to be happy and being happy is being with what I love; a man. At other times, I consistently hear, "You should be with a woman" but that's not want I want. I refuse to play with a woman's mind with head games knowing that my heart is not there. Just because you're living a heterosexual lifestyle doesn't mean you're guaranteed to enter the pearly gates of HEAVEN either.

When I go to church and the Pastor is preaching about homo-sexuality, I feel bad and it makes me fight with myself. Depending on how they deliver their sermon, it makes me feel degraded and at other times I feel convicted. Sometimes I feel that I will never be completely happy because I am gay but at other times I feel that I will. Growing up I never wanted to be gay but that was the feeling that I had, I loved boys instead of girls although I knew my mother didn't want her son to be gay.

My mother instilled in me as a child that being gay was going to be the hardest part of my life. She told me I would have to fight constantly because people would not understand or accept me. I never understood what she meant by that as a child or a teenager. Living in today's world, I fully understand what she was talking about because some people can be straight cruel and hurtful. Some heterosexuals don't consider the fact that gay people have feelings too. I bleed just like the next person but I was gay so my life would be so much different.

I wish I had grown up reading the bible so I would have a clearer understanding about it, unfortunately I didn't but I read it today. At times I am still confused but I just want to be happy and I know for me, being happy is with a man and not a woman, no one wants their heart played with.

I decided to get married to Price because I felt that we were in love with each other. I thought that I would be spending the rest of my life with him. Had I known then what I know now, I don't think I would change a thing. I am so blessed to have even experienced what I did while in that relationship. It was my very first relationship and it taught me a lot.

That relationship taught me mostly that Karma is real, but even the Bible says, "You reap what you sow," It's so true and it happened to me. I definitely reaped what I had sown with Price. I still want to be in a relationship with a man but as far as marriage, I want to get to know him first this time unlike I did with Price.

The hurt that I experienced in that relationship alone was too much for me and the thought of even going through that again is something that I can't fathom. Going forward I just want to be in a committed relationship before marriage.

It's very hard to live a happy life being gay because I am always judged so in a way I can't be who I really am. I have to be different sometimes in certain situations because it could be an important matter and I wouldn't want to jeopardize my future, sometimes I just feel so torn.

My sister and Pastor Rickie Rush came into my life strong at the perfect time. I was going through a valley experience and mu sister taught me more about GOD than I had ever known and Pastor Rush explained some of the chapters in the Bible during his services on Sunday's at IBOC (Inspiring Body of Christ Church) in Dallas, Texas.

I learned that the benefit of my suffering was building my character and helping others in the process. I was spewing out to others everything that I was learning. I wanted people to feel what I felt about GOD. I didn't turn my back on GOD but I definitely strayed away, not because I was GAY but because I felt like so much had happened to me and I had suffered beyond my belief. I learned that "If GOD brings you to it, he shall bring you through it" and all my sufferings would come to pass. I never cursed GOD but just constantly asked, "Why me?" But still, I believed, with all that I've been through I still believe!

******

I didn't want to be like most gay men, playing the game of "Don't Ask Don't Tell." Living in Atlanta I've learned that having HIV means nothing to a lot of men, both gay and straight. I've encountered so many here and no one had a problem with me having it. I divulged my status because I didn't care and in return others would only say that they have dated someone before who has HIV. No one really admitted to having HIV, they simple didn't care. It was just like we were in the Army and playing the game, "Don't Ask, Don't Tell."

If I didn't bring it up, neither did they. I felt obligated to tell every person that tried to talk to me on a sexual level about my status. It never mattered to them at all and not even that I had a boyfriend, no one cared. That scared me more than ever because there were other diseases floating around too.

Atlanta is also the hot spot for Syphilis. I was scared as hell and I made a promise to myself that anyone I dated, we would have to get tested together if they were not willing to tell me their health issues upfront. I didn't trust a soul with my body anymore. Hell, I was just married to someone who was fucking just about everyone he had met RAW. **Message**

Price was so fine that I really don't know if he told people his status.

I was really all too familiar with "Don't Ask Don't Tell." It was all around me within my own community; the gay community that is. Bernard didn't tell me when he raped me that he had FULL BLOWN AIDS, nor did Price tell me when he first tested Positive! I saw a copy of the medical papers that he gave to the doctor while I was making them 4 trips back and forth from Cali to Dallas.

That was when I learned that Price had tested positive for Syphilis again and the papers stated that he tested Positive for HIV a totally different date than what he initially told me. Within the time that he told me, we fucked 2 weeks straight like jack rabbits, raw and he came in me every single time! I knew that I was going to be with him so I didn't care to have unprotected sex with him.

The law requires people that have HIV/AIDS to disclose their status to their sexual partner. The only problem with most gay men like Price is they have too many sexual partners to narrow it down to the person that infected them.

******

CHAPTER 8

A NEW LOVE WITH #26

When I finally got my heart back together from the many pieces that Price left it in and the desire to move on it was extremely hard. For one, I had major trust issues but I learned to open the door and allow my guard to come down; some. I didn't want to lose sight of what I wanted from my mate this go round. Everything that Price lacked in, the new love would have more of. The dating process was going to be even harder for me I had thought at first.

I wasn't worried about my looks because I knew I was very attractive but disclosing my HIV status was going to be kind of hard because that is the type of information that you just didn't divulged to someone all at once but I learned to just be upfront rather beating around the bush and hoping that they would say that they have it first. There are not too many people that will do that in this world. There are some, but not a lot.

I was now living in Atlanta, GA. The state that was known for three things; DL brothers, their high HIV rates and gay men.

Basically I would fit right in. I had mostly slept with DL men in my past, I was now living with HIV and I was gay.

The saying is, "Don't go looking for love, let it find you." That's exactly what happened when I least expected it on May 6, 2011. Of course my new Kia took me to the limits and with my driving record I was pulled over the second day after I got it. FUCK! I was doing 65 in a 35 mph zone. I was looking out my side view mirror when this fine ass cop comes walking to my driver side door.

Excuse me, what's your rush? You do know your were doing 65 in a 35 mph zone right? That is considered reckless driving!

Blonde moment No officer, I was not paying attention and I just purchased this vehicle right off the assembly line yesterday and I was using the pedals on the steering wheel and I didn't even see the speed limit posted, while I was gazing into them damn hazel eyes.

Step out the car please, sir.

FUCK, I'm about to go to jail I immediately thought.

He placed me in the back of the squad car and began asking me questions.

There was my weakness sitting right in front of me through a damn wired gate in a patrol car and it was a Dodge Charger too. He was my height, 5'8", my size, 150 pounds, pure red bone heaven. When he looked in my eyes and my eyes locked with his, it happened all over again, I was stuck. He was mixed with Jamaican and black and I knew it right off the bat when he spoke. That accent captured my heart and he introduced himself before I could even say my name. I was still stuck on the way he spoke.

WOW! Was this really happening to me? I felt like I had to tell him right away that I was HIV Positive but I didn't. Then the questions came rolling off his tongue like he saw within my soul.

Where are you from sexy man and what's your name? Are you single?

WHAT THE FUCK, I was shell shocked like the ninja turtles. I began to stutter because I was stuck. He was a damn cop and he was gay or DL to my knowledge. This was the first encounter that I had, had with a man in a long time after Price. This couldn't be happening because I told myself love was not living here anymore. Before I knew it, I was answering questions and giving answers that he hadn't asked and asking questions before I could even give him a chance to reply.

I am from Gary, Indiana but spent half of my life in Minnesota. I am single and I just got out of a relationship and I'm not even looking for another one. I also come with a tremendous amount of baggage just a FYI!

Damn! He responded.

We both laughed.

Then I said it. I am also HIV Positive so if you want, please walk away now.

"What the fuck", he said. Why would I walk away? Most men would never say that off the bat.

I'm not most men. I just felt like I needed to tell you that because I don't want to go down the road that I've already been down.

I would love to get to know you on a personal level. You seem like a nice, cool honest guy.

Thank you kid.

Kidd? I'm 28 years old.

That was just a figure of speech man.

We both laughed again

I'm 32 going on 33 December 15th.

Cool, I'll be 29 June 26th.

Hhhmmm, we are only five years apart. I was thinking to myself that was a good sign because that means that we both know what we already want and we both have probably already been through some bad relationships.

I'm a Personal Trainer, Film Editor and Police Officer with Atlanta's Finest.

YYYYEEEESSSS!!!!! That's all I needed to hear. A man with a CAREER. POW

Well a little about me, I own rental property back home, currently just finished my first book and I am retired at 32.

This was not happening to me. My dream man was right in front of my face. He was a red bone, mixed with black and Jamaican, has a career and he didn't walk away after I said I was HIV Positive. WAIT! Something wasn't adding up.

So what's your status I asked?

I'm HIV Negative.

WTF. And why would you even want to get to know me?

He said, my mother always taught me, "Everyone comes with something and no one is perfect." I practice safe sex and we would just have to be careful if we ever went there.

Side Stare let's go get tested tomorrow together I replied.

He said what time will you be ready? I'll come and pick you up and then we could do dinner afterwards, my treat.

I Flat Lined

Pick me up around noon. Wait, maybe a little after 1 pm, I'm never on time.

Got you, it's a date then!

Then he let me out the back of the squad car and I went back to my car with butterflies all in my stomach. I felt like Gloria in

"Waiting to Exhale" while I walked away I thought "Is he watching me?"

And when I turned around he was still standing outside his patrol car "Watching Me!" All I could do was smile and throw up two fingers, but in actuality I really wanted to scream.

All that night while with Avern, I couldn't stop talking about him. I couldn't even remember his damn name because I was so excited, so I just started calling him #26. My best friend was very supportive but over protective also. He didn't want to see me hurt again. He insisted on meeting this new guy to see if he could get a feel for him before I got too wrapped up. I told him to be at my house before noon the next day just in case #26 showed up early.

The next day came and I was up early and ready before Avern even got there. This was truly a first for me and I knew I was over excited. Avern saw that in me also and said, "Bitch you is too giddy over this dude, calm down before you run him off!" We both laughed and smoked before #26 arrived. Then my doorbell rang and I had Avern let him in because I was nervous. They introduced themselves and chatted for a minute while I acted like I was getting ready up stairs.

I started coming down the stairs so #26 stood, looked at me like he was standing to greet the president entering a ball room. He said, "You look beautiful." I politely mumbled the words, "Thank you" but couldn't get them out without breaking a smile. Once I got to the bottom of the steps he met me there with the warmest hug and handed me beautiful bouquet bearing an assortment of two dozen beautiful roses. I had completely shut the rest of my condo out of view and I all I saw was him. I was flabbergasted and speechless. Then he said, "Are you ready?" I said, "Yep" and we walked out the door and Avern came behind us and closed it.

I didn't know which car was his once we got outside into the parking lot and he said, "I parked right next to you." WOW, he had the new 2011 Dodge Charger. It was the same color as my Kia. He opened my door and then he got in and leaned in for the kiss. WHEW, I flat lined all over again and my heart was jumping out of my chest. He then started smiling and said was that too much? I said nope and kept smiling.

On the way riding to the clinic we had a very long conversation. He asked everything from the sun up to the sun down. I was nervous as fuck like I was getting tested for the first time and I had already known my results. I guess I was nervous for him. Although it really didn't matter whether he was Negative or Positive, I still wanted to get to know him. Fuck that, I wanted to be with him, it just felt so right.

We walked into the clinic, sat down and filled out the paperwork and then after we were finished, he took my clipboard back to the receptionist and she asked, "Will this be separate or together?" He said no, it will be together and he pulled out his credit card and said, "Please charge it." I know when he looked back, he saw every teeth in my damn mouth. I was too through. She explained that our results would be back within 20 minutes after the procedure was over so we could wait or come back. He told her that we would come back after we were done.

We went across the street and had lunch at Red Lobster while waiting for our results. Although I knew what my results would be, I still was nervous for him. In my mind I wanted him to be Positive because I didn't want to go through the guilt of him being Positive later if he was indeed negative. At the same time I was elated that someone was still willing to date me knowing that I was Positive and they were Negative.

After we returned to the clinic our results were available. Sure enough, #26 wasn't lying; he was HIV Negative but I was still HIV Positive. **Side Stare** He saw the look on my face and said it didn't matter because he liked me for me and not for what I had. Those words will never leave my mind. I could still hear his voice saying that until this very day. I then began to cry because that was so heart felt. He had touched me in a way that no one could. I had fallen in love all over again at the moment that I thought I never would.

******

You know my cycle, something good was always followed by something bad and the devil had crept back into my home before I even knew it. I began talking to Price again by late November of 2011. All the feelings that I thought were gone came rushing back, just in a different way. I still loved him because he was my first love and I couldn't shake it.

I, myself being the new person that I was, could not play two sides of the fence. So I broke it off with #26 thinking that I could still salvage my marriage. #26 Was devastated and came over to the house to talk to me and see if he had did or said something wrong to make me want to give up on my new found love. I had to be honest and tell him exactly why rather than beating around the bush and coming up with some lame ass excuse. So I told him the truth, "I was still in love with my ex."

After he cried in my arms the same exact way that I did with Price, I told him that I still wanted to be his friend and that I didn't want to lose that part of our relationship. To my surprise, he insisted that we stay friends also. He told me not to get my hopes up high because Price was not the right person for me nor could Price ever love me genuinely. We remained friends all while I still was trying to make my marriage work over the damn phone.

******

I felt all types of ways for my husband. I was angry, bitter, hurt and yet kind of sort still in love. I still felt that I couldn't trust him but despite that I still wanted to continue. The first sign that it wasn't going to work with Price and I was when Price called me on December 2nd, 2011 around midnight stating that he had just had a car accident and needed some money to pay his car insurance bill because he didn't pay it and his insurance was about to lapse. Really? I said, "Damn dude, we only been talking for a little over a month and your calling asking for money already?" He had the damn nerves to tell me that we were still married and I was obligated to help him. I felt obligated to hang up in his damn face and that's just what the fuck I did after I said, "Hell Naw!"

We didn't speak anymore until the day of my birthday. He sent a text message first saying, "Happy Birthday Bae." Of course that put a smile on my face and it made me call him. We spoke for about thirty minutes but Avern was signaling me to hang up because we were supposed to be getting ready to go out to celebrate my birthday with some friends who were meeting us at the club. After we said our goodbyes I hung up with a huge smile on my face. Avern said very sarcastically, "Girl give it up, that was all just game to pull you back in." I didn't have anything to say back because in my heart I knew Avern was right.

Within the next thirty minutes my phone was ringing again. I was upstairs in the bathroom and I had just got out the shower. Avern answered my phone and said it was some boy on the phone and he was crying. I said, "Look at the number bitch and see who it is." Avern said, "No name came up." So I asked what the number was. He then said "Bitch if you don't come get this phone and hurry your slow ass up!"

I made it to the phone and some boy was crying and asked was this Sam? I said yes it is and who is this very sarcastically. I didn't know the number nor the voice and to top it off it was a Chicago number. He then said, "This is Arius. You don't know me but I have been dating Price since January of this year and we just broke up tonight." Are you serious? I thought, instead I just said "Okay." He calmly then said "I'm not calling you to start anything but I just want to know one thing." I said, "Okay" again, "Go ahead."

Arius wanted to know why did Price and I break up and did he ever hit me. I told him simply, "Price cheated and yes he did." His reply was just "WOW!" He said Price told him that I was the one who cheated and took everything after he caught me cheating in Dallas, Texas. He went on to say that Price told him, "I never put my hands on Samuel in anger." However we just had an argument and he was about to hit me.

He said that he took Price phone while Price was packing his clothes to leave his house and got my number out of it before he left. I told him that I would have to call him back the next day because I was about to go out to the club. He said, "Happy Birthday and enjoy yourself and please don't forget to call me tomorrow." **Side Stare** this dude knew my birthday? I hung up wondering how much false and true information that Price divulged to Arius about me. I knew everything was happening all over again and this time we weren't even in the same damn state.

The next morning I called Arius back even though I had a hang-over. I enjoyed my birthday to the point of no return but my mind was still roaming thinking about Price, #26 and Arius.

They were together since January?

Wasn't I just with Price in July (not sexually) and he was trying to come back to Atlanta with me?

Didn't his mother just say she thought Price was going back home to Atlanta with me?

My mind was running wild while Arius line was ringing. "Hey Sam," he said as he answered the phone. Hey Arius, what's going on and how is your morning I asked. Arius then began to tell me about my husband and his cheating ways. Price had fucked just about all his friends too and everyone he was running with. Go figure. That was not a surprise to me at all. He then said the thing that brought me to tears. "Price had you set up love." I knew in my heart that he did but I had no solid proof. Arius told me what type of car the boys drove that robbed and beat me, how many men there were and even that I was at a gas station. I almost lost my damn mind, all I could do was cry. The person that I fell in love with really tried to have me killed all because his ass was the one cheating and I left him. WOW.

I couldn't even hear anymore and I knew Arius wasn't lying. I hadn't posted any of the details like that on face book and we were not Facebook friends nor was my book even out. Furthermore, I didn't go into detail like that even in my book so how could he have even known this information, Price had to tell him. I was livid.

After we'd spoken the entire morning until a little after 1pm that afternoon, I hung up pissed but relieved. I knew now if I didn't know then, to just move the fuck on and let that sorry ass motherfucker go. This low life bum bitch was still playing the same fucking games and now he is playing them with someone else, so another person is walking away felling exactly how I felt. To top things off, Price left Arius and went to stay with a mutual friend they had.

Damn, the cycle just continues as he had left me before and went and stayed with Marquise while we were living in Minnesota which was also a mutual friend.

Surprisingly, the next morning Price called me and was talking all sweet as I listened to his bullshit ass story of how him and his "bestie" had stopped being best friends and had gotten into it after he had spoken to me. I told him to hold on while I clicked over and called Arius. I told Arius to be quite and just listen. Then I clicked back over and told Price to continue with his story. I let him talk and tell all his lies while I had a look on my face that he couldn't see through the phone. If he'd been in front of me, I think I probably would have killed him or beat his ass to a pulp like he was a damn stranger.

After he was finish talking, he asked me why was I so quite. And before I knew it, the "Rage of Carrie" was released out of me and I snapped. LITERALLY! I lost it on his ass and to my surprise he didn't hang up. I think he wanted to hear what I actually had to say. Needless to say, after I was done, Arius started going in and before I knew it, we were all arguing. Then Price said, "fuck you bitches and that's why I used both of y'all ass and got everything that I wanted and y'all are mad because I was fucking other people and y'all friends." Arius tried to go in but I told him to be quite because I had this one.

My reply was simply, "Bitch at the end of the day, you still a bum ass nigga, living from pillar to post, with no pot to piss in nor a window to throw it out of, to top that off you're a fucking bottom that just had scabies, now run tell that!" Then he hung up, and that was the last time we spoke.

******

I was still speaking to #26 daily and I had told him what happened. He surprised me again, by not saying I told you so. Instead he hugged me and said, "You can cry on my shoulder baby" in his Jamaican voice. Ironically I didn't even want to cry because I wasn't even mad at this point. I was completely over Price and that was a total shock in itself.

I did however lean on #26 shoulder and apologized for even thinking that I could have a love that was lost. #26 said, "Baby you had to go through that again to know for sure that he was not the right person for you." #26 had his own; own car, own house, and most of all he had a career; he was a police officer so I knew he wasn't out to try and get something from me. To top all that off, I'm the one living with HIV.

******

While #26 and I were getting our relationship back on track, Lucciano had just returned to Chicago from West Virginia. He was doing great and we kept in contact over the months after I saw him last in the hospital.

In fact, Lucciano, Arius and myself actually all began to talk over the phone daily after my first conversation with Arius. It was surprising that Price had no effect on our lives and we had all moved on. We were all building a bond that no one could ever imagine. Damn, I was now friends with my ex's ex Lucciano before me and Arius, the ex after me. Now this would be some crazy shit to other people looking in from the outside.

In February 2011, the week of the 5th, I was scheduled to be in Minnesota for my first television and radio interview for my book. We had all planned to meet that weekend in Chicago and finally just kick it. I was floored when I saw them both. I was happy because we were all doing well despite our setbacks. We all hugged each other and started smiling at one another looking at how we were all different from each other but yet the same. Two things in particular stood out overall. We all were born in December: Lucciano and I with the same birthday and Arius' a couple of days after ours, we're all HIV Positive.

We cruised around the city in my KIA and I was introduced as the husband of the ex to both sides of their families and the author of "Eyes Without A Face." Surprisingly, both of them were spreading the word to everyone in Chicago about my book and I was collecting money from their family and friends although the books weren't available at the time.

Later that night before going to the club, Price's aunt must have seen one of my posts that I was in Chicago and called and asked me to stop by. The three of us went over to visit Price's aunt, she knew Arius and Price were once together but hadn't met Lucciano, nor did she have any idea that we knew each other let alone were hanging together. She was surprised.

When Price's little cousin, his aunts son, opened the door his eyes got real big and he screamed, "It's Sam!" and gave me the warmest hug ever. He was so happy to see me and I was even happier to see him. Then he screamed, "It's Arius too!" He then gave Arius a hug. I was happy to see that Arius had a connection with Price's little cousin the same way I did.

Upon entering the apartment, Price's aunt was so shocked to see us all together after I said this is Lucciano; the one before me which she had heard so much about that you could have sworn she'd seen a ghost. We just burst out laughing. She said, "Boy, if Price was here to see this!" Then Arius said, "Here we are, the 1st, 2nd and 3rd." Price's aunt said, "No, more like the 8th, 9th and no one will ever know what number you may be," to Arius. That just let me know how much of a whore this dude really was if his aunt knew his ways.

Price's aunt then called his mother and told her I was there. Price's mom and I had a solid relationship, I'd looked at her as my own mother because I didn't have my mother's love like Price had his. My mother-in-law came and we chatted, smoked and before long, I said I had to go. My mother-in-law asked if I had seen her son. I said while looking in her eyes with a hard stare, "No, and I don't even want too!" After that, we all hugged and the three of us left.

It was time to party after that visit. We all went back to Lucciano's house where we changed clothes and Arius friends came to Lucciano's and we all met each other. It was five cars and every car had three to four people in it. We were deep and ready to tear up Chicago. Lucciano paid my way into the club and Arius paid for my drinks all night. I felt like these were the best friends because of how we all were connected. They were not fake or fucked my husband behind my back like my other so called friends but they had their time with him.

The night the next morning, I was off to Gary, Indiana before heading back home to Atlanta. I enjoyed that time spent with my new friends and our bonds are even stronger today. While in Chicago, I never saw Price and I didn't want to either. I was so over that asshole, I was finally the one throwing up my two fingers; "DUCES BITCH!"

******

After about a month #26 and I were going strong and I completely gave myself to him. February 14, 2012, Valentine's Day was so romantic. He had a hotel room at the Westin Hotel, downtown Atlanta, the seventieth floor with rose petals all over the room. Petals of passionate red and friendship yellow with every step, there must have been twelve dozen blanketing the room in a velvet comforter. The sound of smooth jazz filled the air with flickering candles lining the Jacuzzi and bed. Before long we sank into the warm water of the Jacuzzi gazing into each other's eyes as we massaged feet, drank champagne and talked. The inevitable reward for preparing such a romantic evening culminated in throbbing passion and pleasure.

I was completely free of Price and I wanted to love and be loved again by someone real, #26 gave me everything I wanted; mentally, spiritually, physically, romantically and even financially. He gave me his all and I was singing Beyoncé's "Love on top" the next morning when I woke up without the radio. More importantly he knew I was not going to lose myself in love with him and that I put GOD first this time.

In so many ways #26 reminded me of Gary. I knew Gary really loved me and that's why this time I wasn't going to let #26 go. When I sang my songs by Keisha Cole, Mary J. Blige, Brandy or Jennifer Hudson, instead of sarcastically turning his head, he told me to go higher. Hell, I didn't think I could sing, I just thought I screamed but he loved it. Furthermore, he loved Tabby (my cat, my baby, my child) and Tabby loved him. #26 Became my soul mate I loved him and he loved me and accepted me, flaws and all. I had finally found someone to unpack all the baggage that I came with.

CHAPTER 9

ADONIS IS BACK

The last time I had heard from Adonis was in April of 2008 and now exactly four years later in April of 2012 he's back in my life. I was on Facebook when he hit me up. He still lives in Baltimore but he's now married to a Spanish chick, their wedding was in August of 2008 right after I'd married Price. I still could not fathom the fact that he had gotten married, let alone, had been married for the last four years, part of me was jealous inside. I wanted to be with him but he couldn't live the life that I wanted, an openly gay lifestyle. I wanted the same relationship with Adonis that I had with Price. But that was not going to happen.

Before long I was talking to Adonis every day and building plans to cheat with him. When the opportunity came we decided it was time to see each other. We had planned to meet in May while #26 was in New York City with his family and just like that, Adonis arrived the next morning. Then I found myself back to being number two while I was still number one with #26.

He was overly excited to see me and I was equally as excited to see him. Let me quit lying; I was elated. I wanted this so badly, for the past four years I'd dreamt of being in his arms just like old times. As soon as he departed on his early bird flight, he called. I was already waiting at the baggage claim outside the airport. I had just dropped #26 off and I circled the terminal for an additional thirty minutes to see Adonis but it felt like an eternity. We talked on the phone from the time he got off the tram to him walking out those doors. He only had a carry-on bag because he only stayed the weekend.

As soon as Adonis came out those doors, I was already waiting on the sidewalk. We embraced so hard. I smelled him before he even walked up. To my surprise we both cried as we hugged each other. I was not expecting him to cry. We must have hugged for over 10 minutes, it felt like heaven, I thought I was dreaming. I didn't want to let him go. Every moment we'd ever shared ran through my mind in those 10 minutes. I loved him with every ounce of blood in my body.

We got in the car and hugged again. Before we drove off I said, "I love you mane, I love you so much!" At that point he looked into my eyes and told me that he loved me too, that was all I needed to hear. With those few words he put me at ease. The last time he had told me he loved me was right before he moved back to Baltimore four years ago. He was married and I was in relationship. We never said we were going to have sex over the phone at all. We just wanted to see each other, talk about the old times, and embrace one another.

We went out to eat, the movies, bowling, we did a lot of talking, I read my book to him and we held each other. I had already told Adonis about my situation, he understood HIV and was not turned off or scared. I just enjoyed us spending time together. I massaged him and he massaged me. That Saturday night while he held me and fell asleep, I cried. I cried myself to sleep because I knew it would be a long time before we would ever see each other again.

I was glad for the memories and the fact that I was back in his arms, but I didn't want it back the way that it was going. I would have to be single and so would he.

I think the majority of the weekend was him expressing his thoughts about my book. He didn't want to read it, halfway through the first chapter he broke down. He said he never knew about my past because I had never opened up to him about it, actually I never really spoke of my past until I wrote the book. All he knew was my family in Minnesota and that I was from Gary, other than that I never said anything.

Instead of him reading, he asked could I read it to him. That was a hard task for me because every time I read it, I cried or it put me back into that dark place where I was, but for him I read it. We laughed at times, and cried at others. I watched him as he covered his eyes wet with tears, then he'd hold me and at other times and just kept whispering in my ear, "I love you Sam!" When I got to Price's chapter, his pain and other feelings went completely out the door. He was now enraged.

Adonis was pissed off that I had gone through that with Price. He was baffled at how I tolerated so much. I put the book down and explained to him how deeply in love I was. I had to make him understand that Price was completely gay. Basically, I was telling Adonis that Price had no problem with showing me affection in public. He had no problem with others knowing that we were together and I had thought that he loved me for me. Adonis still wasn't buying it. He hated Price and hadn't even met him. I told him that #26 felt the same exact way as he did. Adonis said, "If #26 don't feel the way I feel, I would have said leave his ass right now!" He was happy that someone loved me the way he did. Adonis said, "All I want is for you to be happy dude, that's all!" I needed to hear that, I needed all kinds of confirmation from him. #26 Was my first relationship after two years of not being with Price. I told Adonis I was scared, I was angry at times, and often confused. I felt like I was living in a dream because #26 was so good to me. He was beyond the best relationship that I'd ever had. But I knew within time I was going to fuck it up.

I told Adonis that one thing I learned from being with Price was that you can't enter a new relationship if your still hurting from the previous one. I knew that I still had feelings for my husband and although he didn't want me, at times I still wanted him. I had to be honest with myself as well as others. I was just tired of lying to people and lying to myself. I took a vow that meant more to me than anything in the world.

Before I knew it, I broke down. Adonis held me as I cried. My feelings were still torn. I had not gotten over my husband at that point. Although he betrayed me in the worst ways possible, I still loved him. As I continued to read, Adonis was getting more upset and right at the end of the book after I closed it, he started asking where Price was. He wanted to see him badly.

I was not like Price though, I wasn't saying anything, not even that Price was in Chicago. Adonis had an Army background and had been in battle in Iraq. He was now ready for war and I would see a part of Adonis that I'd never seen, nor wanted to see. When I say Adonis was pissed I mean he was ready to kill somebody, he was enraged. I had to calm him down quickly. I think his PTSD kicked in and he felt every feeling that I had felt after waking up in the hospital room.

After calming him down, we went for a walk around my complex. I told him that I had forgiven my husband and I had moved on from that evil part of my life. There was simply nothing I could do. He asked did anyone get caught and that's when it truly hit me. I had been lying to all my family and friends about that part of the situation.

******

I was so afraid of that situation that when they were caught in Dallas the following year of April 2011, I couldn't even identify them. I had driven all the way to Dallas with Avern and pictured those men in my mind the entire ride. When I walked into the Dallas Police Department and spoke with the detective, all the images in my mind went blank. I was scared as hell. I pictured myself in the back seat of the car I was currently driving.

I saw them attack me. I heard their voices. I felt their bodies. However, when the detective showed me the pictures of the men that they had arrested, the images of them were completely gone. The police were looking at me crazy as hell but I couldn't remember what they looked like to save my life. I was then taken to the room to point them out in a line up. I was looking at six men right in front of me. One of the six men was right in front of my face and I couldn't pick him out. The detective told them to turn to the left. My heart dropped.

All I could hear was, "Bitch you are about to die so say your prayers!" Right then and there, I started praying and crying. I couldn't remember what he looked like and just like that, they exited the room to the right. Then right after that, the next set of six men came in and again, I went blank. I don't know if I was just scared as hell or did I really have memory loss. Either way, the men that tried to kill me over my husband were about to walk scot-free within the next couple of hours and there was nothing that I could do about it.

I was hurt, angry, sad, scared and confused all at the same time. I was thinking, "How in the hell could I forget them!" I had been dreaming of these mother fuckers and now was my chance to get revenge by taking their freedom but the joke was on me. My cycle was beginning; something good was always followed by something bad. The bad guys had been caught and it was time for them to serve justice but I couldn't identify them to make that possible. So they walked!

I felt so ashamed and embarrassed that I had told all my family and friends that they had been caught and were serving time. I didn't want anyone to know the truth.

******

Adonis understood why I did what I did and because of his understanding I was willing and felt that I had to tell my family and friends the truth too. Everyone deserved to know. I also told Adonis that when I did speak with Price, I made it my business to always tell him that they were serving time and he knew who they were. I was always hoping that he would say a name. However, he never did so I had to put that behind me. That's one of the hardest things that I had ever done other than trying to move on from my marriage but I serve a mighty GOD and he was helping me along the way.

Adonis and I will always remain close. We shared a bond for nine months with no arguing. He and #26, will always be the two men who got away. I had something that I had always dreamed of; the perfect men that looked straight. I believe that since I was having sex as a child with older straight men, that I adapted to having a straight man as my man. I was not and have never been attracted to men that were known gay men. They just seemed to always carry some type of feminine trait that I couldn't take.

Hell, I couldn't tell #26 was gay until he told me. Adonis was a straight man and I thought I was in heaven while I was with him. However, Price was the 1st gay man that I dated and took that relationship even further. After that was over, I was left with the perception that gay male relationships would never work. Lesbians had more longevity than gay men, and that's a fact!

CHAPTER 10

I WANTED A BABY

As I told you before, the first woman, well girl I had sex with, was when I was 13 years old. I didn't like it one bit, plus she gave me gonorrhea. It wasn't until moving to Minnesota and while I was prostituting that I began to have sex with women again. The only difference is this time around I was being paid money to do it, and money talked and anything else was just bullshit. I always had women coming at me saying how they could turn me back straight but they never knew that I was never straight. Being GAY was who I am. It's not a choice for me. The only thing was, I wanted a baby bad as hell, and I knew the only way to get one, was to have sex with women.

While prostituting and on runs, the call came in to the Boss for a brown skinned brother, around 5'8, slim build, well-endowed and good looking. Well that was me all the way needless to say. We had other people on our team but that was my description to the tee.

The first woman to pay me was a Caucasian woman, around 200 pounds, with long blonde hair and she was married with 2 kids. She wanted 2 hours with me which was $3,200.00 total and $2,000.00 for my cut. Remember my split with the Boss was 60/40 my way. If I played my cards right, and went hard, I even got a tip on the side that was all mine.

I already knew what she wanted which was just to give me head and she wanted to get fucked right. She wanted some hood dick per her phone call to the Boss. My Boss already knew that I was the right person for her.

Hood dick- generally a black man that fucks and takes the pussy or ass in an aggressive way without raping the person

Once I walked into that hotel room at the Hilton downtown Minneapolis I was well prepared. I knew I was dealing with someone who had money because she had a suite on the top floor. I had drink in my system and I smoked 2 hydro blunts. My dick was hard as a rock and I was ready to please her. We chatted for a couple of minutes and she went into depth about how she wanted to get fucked and she wanted to make sure her pussy was extra wet to take it all. After I pulled down my pants and she started giving me head, I started playing with her pussy and titties. She was so wet, she reminded me of Morton's salt, "When it rain it pours," she was running like it was raining.

After we laid down she was moaning and saying how she wanted me to eat her pussy. **Real Hard Blank Stare** I didn't eat pussy and never had until that night. I told her that I didn't and she said the magic words that I wanted to hear. "I will pay you more. PLEASE?" No more encouragement was needed, I was all about the money and before I knew it I was performing oral sex. I was uncomfortable and at one point I had to take a break and wash my face, I went back at it like I'd never left. I was hitting it from every position possible like I had just gotten out of jail. I wanted her to cum as many times as she could because I was never going to cum. I didn't even feel the urge to bust a nut. Mostly because I was trying my best to fuck her for more than 2 hours and I succeeded. I fucked that woman for 3-1/2 hours total and still didn't bust. I had her begging for me to stop.

Once we stopped, we laid there and talked some more and she told me what she did and what her husband did. She said her name was Becky. I was in her head and I wanted to know what her income was. I was definitely about to make her my regular fuck buddy. After she said she ran branches for a bank and her husband was a CEO of a company and that they stayed in Ham Lake Minnesota in a mini mansion, I knew that meant a mansion. She said she needed some good dick on a regular basis and I let her know I was going to be the one to give it to her without hesitation whenever she wanted it.

After we showered together and I washed her off, she began to just melt apart in my arms. Afterwards, I held her and we both got dressed. She then went into her Dooney & Bourke purse and pulled out the cash which was in all 100 dollar bills. She paid me a total of $5,000.00. I got $4,800.00 for three hours and a $200.00 tip. After I went back to the Boss's house, I walked away with $3,200.00. I knew she was going to be my "Come up." Out of all the tricks I turned, the men paid plus tips, but the women were paying the most because of the time being spent.

The next go round was about the same thing except I put it down so good the first time I didn't have to eat the pussy anymore. She was automatically wet just seeing me come into that room. When we finished we had a good conversation and this is when she told me she wanted to bring in her sister and best friend the next time. WOW! I told her I was down but she could not let Boss know. I knew in my head I was about to make a killing and I didn't want to split that money. So I gave her my number and told her to hit me up when she was ready.

To my surprise she called like 2 days later. She was more ready than I was. I didn't even ask what they looked like and frankly I didn't give a fuck. Money was all I saw and I was about to get it. I explained to her that the rate was still the same $3,200.00 for 2 hours and $1,600.00 for every additional hour. She told me that was no problem at all. After I hung up I think I screamed "Cha Ching like about two or three times or maybe even four or five!"

We met back up at the Hilton in the same room. It was like she had this particular room reserved or something. When I walked in, I saw all three of them half way naked in their nighties with no bras or panties on. They were all kind of heavy set weighing 200 pounds or a little more or a little less, with huge breasts (not that I liked them at all) and had long hair; and two were blond and the other a red head. I was about to get it in and make that money.

Before I knew it, they had undressed me while sucking my dick, kissing all over my body and all saying how they wanted my huge cock so badly. They were all sucking on my dick and slapping their face with it, kissing it and sucking on my balls while playing with their pussy and taking off their nighties.

We didn't even make it to the bed before Becky, my main trick was bent over the bed ready for me to run up in her. WHOA, "slow down" I said, "Let me put this magnum on real quick." I wasn't running in nothing raw dog. After I put the condom on I started beating the pussy up doggy style while her best friend was licking her pussy and sucking on my dick and her sister was lying across the bed playing with her pussy. The radio was playing some crazy ass shit but I had completely tuned that out. The only thing I was thinking about was how much money I was about to walk out that door with.

These were some freaks, they were eating, kissing and fingering each other all while I was fucking all of them after a while. Finally I couldn't hold it in no more and I busted after almost close to 2 hours. I still got paid for 2 hours from each of them and walked out with a total of $10,000.00 even! NO FUCKING LIE. They all combined their tips which was a total of $400. Just for me fucking was $9,600.00. And sure as fly's lite on shit, the 3 of them became my regular without Boss ever finding out. Of course from time to time, Becky, my main trick, wanted me to herself once in a while because she was greedy and so was I. Well I was money hungry and I was willing to fulfill her fantasy anyway she wanted it. We were all getting it in 2 to 3 times a week.

My cousin Nina and I moved into a 3 bedroom, 2 full bathroom townhome in Burnsville Minnesota in April of 2002. It came with a fire place, black appliances, and granite counter tops, built in microwave, dishwasher, washer and dryer, and a one car garage, all for $1,100.00 a month. After Nina had her baby, I told her to keep her money for a couple months, and save up, and I paid the rent. I know for a fact that in one year of sex with women and men, plus my regular job, I grossed over $100,000.00, of which a large piece was tax free. **Get yo life look**

Around this time, I was in my early twenties, 22 to be exact, I was working at Tri Advantage along with my cousin Felicia, which was a collection agency. I had just quit my part time job at the credit union because I was not happy. I was pissed that I couldn't get off on some Friday's so I could travel with Jonathan. My boss didn't want to let me off at 3pm and my flights generally left around 5:30. At Tri Advantage I would work from seven to three Monday through Friday so I took that position. It paid less, but I had money saved so I didn't care.

After my second month there, I met a lady named Yvette who was in her early 30's. She was beyond fine, hell I felt she was the one to make me turn straight when I first set eyes on her. She was 5'7", 160 pounds thick, caramel skin tone, nice long hair with weave, but still looked real, pretty brown eyes like my friend Keisha, and had a coca cola shaped body. Every time she saw me, she smiled and called my name. Hey Robert! I would smile and be like, "What's up Yvette!" My cousin introduced me to her because her sister worked there and she told Felicia that Yvette liked me, I was flattered.

I was tricking hard by now and women were more in than men because they paid a lot more. I wasn't going to try to get money from Yvette; I just wanted a bad bitch on my arm. But, I wanted to make sure whoever got that spot light would know my sexuality. Yvette and I began talking on the phone, and hanging out with each other on our lunch breaks. It was while we were eating one day that I dropped the bomb on her. Literally, after I told her, that is exactly what she said.

We were sitting outside in her 2000 something Tahoe 4x4. It was bad as hell, blue, sitting on 22 inch rims with everything included from leather seats to the sun roof she had installed. I will never forget it. We were eating Burger King talking about secrets and our lives when she told me she was a stripper and asked if I had a problem with it. I told her I didn't and I had something a little deeper than that. So I told her that I was bi-sexual. She was like damn, now that was a big bomb you just dropped on me. Yvette went on to say that she had already had a feeling but wasn't for sure. I was thinking of telling her that I was prostituting, but I didn't want to turn her off, so I kept that little secret to myself.

She then stated how much she was feeling me and still wanted to see what could happen. She insisted that she could change me and we would have kids and get married! I laughed because I knew that it was a lie, I liked men; that's it, that's all. But she was so great with my nieces she loved them and they all loved her. I adored how she looked at them and then would look at me sometimes and smile. It actually put me in a vision of me being straight having a family with her.

Yvette and I went on for about three months before she and I had sex. I had waited patiently for that moment. I knew I loved men, but Yvette was the shit and I had to be honest with myself. Plus, I wanted a kid in a bad way. I wanted someone to carry my name. I wanted someone to call my own. I loved my nieces but they were my nieces and not my actual birth children. Hell, the family loved Yvette and my nieces did too, so on that unforgettable night in August of 2002, Yvette and I went out on a date. I will never forget this night.

It was a dream that I had never dreamed before. We went to Benihana Japanese Steakhouse for dinner. We sat there and talked and ate for about two hours and like any other dates we had, she asked for the bill and paid. She never liked me spending money. She told me I was young and needed to save so I was cool with that and I never complained. We were about to go see a movie but somehow Yvette got sidetracked, she wanted to have drinks at her place instead so we left the restaurant and headed back to St. Paul where she lived. She had a beautiful clean place, she was super clean just like me. Yvette had a two story town home that was brand new. She owned her home and everything in it.

I loved that in a woman. I knew she would be a keeper because of everything she portrayed and how she treated me and the girls.

We ended up lying on the couch while I rubbed her legs and feet watching TV, listening to the music and looking at each other. I knew she really liked me and she couldn't stop smiling when we were together which made me smile. We kept telling each other what pretty smiles we have. By this time, a couple hours had gone by and we were out of drinks, I believed we had about four or five each. I know we were really feeling ourselves. She asked me to go upstairs with her to her room.

Once we entered her room, she began kissing me before we could even get to the bed. I was thinking, hell yea, bring this shit on. I was more than ready, I really liked her physically and sexually. My dick was on brick and she knew it. We began undressing each other as she pulled down my pants while I was taking off her shirt. She dropped to her knees and started giving me the best fellatio that this brother has ever had, and I do mean ever had! She sucked on my dick for about twenty minutes none stop. She was licking on my balls, kissing the head of my dick, slapping herself with it and everything. I thought, was this bitch in the room while I sucked dick?! She did it exactly how I had sucked dick and I loved it. So I knew my clients were too. LOL

After that, I pulled her up because I needed a damn break. She was sucking my dick so good, I was about to nut and I was not about to look like no damn fool. I knew how to control myself. I finished taking off the rest of her clothes and laid her against the bed. I kissed her softly from her forehead down to her toes and then spread her legs and went in for that emotional kill. I started eating her pussy and talking to her while looking at her in the face. She was on her back with her legs open and feet up. She maintained eye contact with me until her body began to tremble and thrash about in an uncontrollable orgasm. It was less than fifteen minutes when I felt her moisture and I was shocked when I came up for air looking like a glazed donut. I thought to myself, "Never fucking again will I eat the pussy until she cums!" Yvette came on my face and in my mouth and didn't even bother to tell me to move. Where they do that at? Apparently in St. Paul.

Although I was annoyed, I didn't stop which made it even more intense, and we went at it like two hardened criminals coming off a twenty year lockup without the possibility of parole. I promise we had sex until the sun came up. I held her until we woke up the next morning around 11:00 am. I woke up to Yvette giving me head. After she was done, I just straight smashed.

Yvette was in love with my dick to no return and actually said she was in love with my dick and I could have sex with her when-ever and I wanted. I just needed to hit her up first to make sure we were on. The only bad thing I can say about Yvette and why it would have never worked out between us was because, she had a boyfriend. She was not going to leave him because he was selling drugs big time and he was her personal ATM. However, in due time, she became my personal ATM too.

******

After a couple of years, Becky got me hired at the bank at a higher position so I left the Credit Union. I was making double the salary now and I had my properties. I was out of the game by now but I was still having sex with them from time to time. We eventu-ally became friends. I had met her husband and kids at this point. Her husband thought I was just her gay friend and that's how she wanted it so it was not a problem if we met up late. To this day we are still close. She still asks for it every now and then but I have changed my ways and money can't even buy me to make me go back.

******

During this time I also indulged in a threesome with a married couple. I met the husband first and this dude was off the chain. He was black and Puerto Rican, about 6'3", 190 pounds with curly hair. I met him at a gas station while we were in line paying for gas. I could smell his delicious fragrance in the summer air. I had to ask what he was wearing. He said, "Me?" Then he said just kidding; it's Giorgio Armani. I told him that I loved it. I meant I loved it on him. He said thanks with a slight smile and I knew I could have him right then and there.

When we got outside and started pumping our gas, his car was parked on the opposite side of the pump. He asked me where I was from, how old was I and said his name was "Lewis." YES! I knew he wanted me for sure at this point. I told him that I was 22 going on 23 in a couple of months, from Gary, Indiana and "My name is Trey." He then said, "Cool, nice to meet you, I'm 28 and from Fort Worth, Texas. I've been living here a couple of months with my wife." In the back of my mind I was thinking, this dude is married but that didn't stop me, I still wanted him regardless.

After engaging in small talk he asked if I smoked or drank, "YEP," was my reply. We exchanged phone numbers and he told me to hit him up. The very next day I called him. I was eager to have him and I was not in money mode, at all. I just wanted him to fuck me because he was too fine to let slip away without having.

He gave me his address and told me to roll through and match a blunt with him and his wife. I arrived at his crib around midnight. His Caucasian wife Heidi was blond around 25, skinny and attractive. We all sat on the same couch and watched HBO, smoked and drank. After a while, his wife left the room. While we were alone Lewis began asking me questions like, did I have a girl, what all I got into and if I'd ever done a threesome before? I knew exactly where this was going. My reply was real quick and simple. I have no girl, anything goes and hell yea. Heidi returned a few minutes later wearing bootie shorts and a tank top asking what y'all talking about. "Trey said he gets into everything and he's single too!"

That's when she surprised the hell out of me and instead of sitting back on the couch between us where she originally was, she sat straight on my lap. My dick got immediately hard. Lewis then stood up and pulled down his pants and boxers and she began to suck his dick. Shit, I wanted some too so I put my hands down her shorts and leaned forward and moved her head and started sucking on his dick too. He then ushered us into the bedroom.

We all began to get undressed and he laid down on the bed with his legs spread eagle. She then sat on his face sixty-nine position while I gave him head, as she and I kissed each other and took turns polishing his knob. I started playing with her pussy and she was dripping wet. I don't think I had ever seen someone get tongue fucked the way he was fucking her pussy. I wanted him to tongue fuck my asshole so I told her let's switch, and we did.

I was riding his face like I was in a rodeo. She was sucking his dick like the World was about to end in a couple of minutes, before long she wanted double penetration and you already know I was down, but on the flip side I wanted some dick too and I didn't know if he was going to cum quick after the double penetration. "I want some dick too!" He said, "Cool, no problem there's enough of this 9" pole to go 'round," and he wasn't lying either because his is just as long as mine and slightly more girth. Shit I am not even going to lie, I was wet like a river, I wanted that dick bad. This mother fucker was fine and I had to have it. He grabbed a couple magnum condoms off the night stand, slid one on and gave me one.

Lewis slipped his dick in her asshole. While she was easing her way down I kissed her the entire time and played with her pussy to make her want for both of our poles. After he was completely inside of her, I started working my dick in her pussy. About two minutes later we were completely in both holes. She was moaning like crazy and something happened that I never experienced before. I nutted fast as fuck. FUCK! I couldn't believe that I came that quickly but that shit turned me on. That was my first time with a man and a woman at the same time.

My dick got hard again but quicker than the speed of light. I was inside her wet pussy again before he could say, "Let's switch." We fucked her from every position possible before I came again. All this time, this dude never even busted. He said, alright "Let me fuck you while she suck your dick." I was happy as hell. My turn now bitch, you think you was doing something, now watch me in action, I thought.

Lewis laid on the bed again in the same position this time I worked his dick into my hole and rode it like I was insane. I had that mother fucker moaning and speaking in tongues. I had a habit of looking at the clock while having sex; and before 10 minutes he had let out the loudest moan while she was sucking my dick. That time I didn't cum but the dick was good. I knew for sure that I was going to get that dick again without her around. **Side Stare**

Within a couple months I'd established a real cool relationship with them and it wasn't only about sex when I visited. Sometimes we went bowling, to movie theaters, she'd cook dinner and we even played dominos. Sometimes while she was at work, I was working him. I had him hooked and I knew her schedule like the back of my hand. I even went over on my lunch break if he got off work early just to give him some head.

After a year or so, they moved back to Fort Worth, Texas but we remained cool and kept in contact, they also had a baby a couple of years later too.

******

I knew that every straight man wouldn't get down with every gay man but I figured I could have them all sometimes though. Like I said, I have only been turned down by one man but in reality I knew not to step to some straight men, period. It wasn't like I was in fear that they'd whoop my ass, but some are just too cool.

So another way around that was just to have a threesome with them and some random "Jump off" bitch that wanted two dicks. I was between the ages of 23 and 26 years old and young in my ways. In actuality I slept with those men because I thought I could fill my own empty voids sexually but I never pursued relationships with them. I was too vain at that time in my life; I knew I was the shit and believed that every man felt the same way, at least that's what I was putting out into the atmosphere.

I got a kick out of converting hard core men that claimed they didn't like fags/sissies/punks. I was going to show their asses something different. The sad part is for me it was always so easy. Some straight men are always asking gay men, "Where the bitches at bruh?" It's like they know that us gay men are magnets for girls, which we are for many reasons, that's why they never fail to ask.

They always seem to come with girlfriends, fiancés, and wives or baby mommas. Some are single and just fucking anything moving with a hole; a girl that is. They couldn't care less how she looks, dress or act. I've witnessed some shit in my time of playing that field. I wouldn't consider these men DL but I do think they are very comfortable with their sexuality and only looking to get a nut, but that nut will only be with a woman. They will let a man be present but not let a man touch them; it's strictly a ménage-a-triose.

I think it's a competition and they do too. One reason is that the other men already know that I'm bisexual and not gay, at least that's what I used to tell them. Sometimes I told them that I'm gay which didn't matter to most of them, they wanted to get their nut off and as long as I was not touching them, it really didn't matter what I liked.

The straight man thinks he can fuck better than me just because they are straight and thinks they may have had more pussy than I've had. I've actually had more pussy than most men hands down. I was the all-time professional in that arena. I showed my ass. Every chance I got to fuck around with a straight man and woman I did. That was my world and I was the leader.

******

It all started with a boy named Jay. He was heterosexual and around my age; I was 24 at the time. He was about my height, around 160 pounds, brown skinned, bow legged and a real hood boy. Shit, he lived in the hood too; over in North Minneapolis and had a baby momma. We had a mutual friend named Milan. I always hung around straight men. It was just less problems and I didn't have to worry about the gay men trying to fuck me left and right. I didn't do gay men so there was no need to hang around them like that, I didn't trust them.

Jay always seemed to have a slight attitude when we hung out together. I assumed he hated gay people by the way he'd cut his eyes at me sometimes. His conversation was smooth but he just seemed to always give me the side stare look. Maybe he didn't trust me.

One night while we were all chilling over Milan's, Becky called and wanted to come over to my house. She and her husband had gotten into an argument and she just wanted to get out and have a few drinks. I was out of the escort game so I didn't charger her. I wanted to see if she'd let me bring someone else if he was down too.

I think Milan, had gone to the bathroom upstairs so I made my move. I told Jay I was about to dip. I was going to meet up with this white freak, and he said, "I'm rolling with you," without any hesitation. When Milan came back down stairs, I told him I was about to bounce and Jay said he was too, and I was going to drop him off.

Now remember, I felt that Jay didn't like me. He never got in my car without Milan for one, and now he was talking like a run-a-way train to me but he was so hood with it and it was cute. He was only talking and acting cool because he was about to get some pussy. I was cool with that too. I knew I couldn't have him, but I knew I could at least see what he was working with and how he worked it.

Once we got to my house, Becky was already there sitting in the parked car. Jay and I had already stopped at the liquor store on the way. I had to avoid all the in between shit. When Becky got out the car she had a surprised look on her face she had never had me along with another man, but she didn't back down nor leave. Instead she said, "So I see you went to the liquor store already!" I said, "That's right" very sarcastically but funny. Then she asked "What's your friend's name?"

I knew right then and there she was going to do whatever I wanted her to do. I told her his name was Jay and he spoke and said, "What's up, what's your name?" She told him "Becky", as we walked through the door. I felt like there was nothing else to be said as I closed the door and they were standing in the hall way. I just told them to go to my room which was straight down the hall and to the right. I went in the kitchen and got some glasses for the alcohol.

I walked into the room, they were already sitting on the bed with their shoes off and she looked like she was ready. I turned on the TV with a porno, mostly for extra light in the room. We drank and talked for like fifteen minutes before I started rubbing on Becky getting her hot and ready, then Jay looked at me and I gave him that "Nicca, you better do something" look! He started rubbing on her and she started whispering "Trey," and she squirmed from side to side as we were rubbing her and taking off her clothes.

After she was completely naked, I started coming out of my clothes, my pants first. Jay was coming out of his clothes too. I saw him look up at me for a second but he kept undressing. We were all butt ass naked on my bed and I started kissing Becky while Jay was playing with her pussy. Before I knew it, this nicca was eating her out. I was shocked as hell but he was tearing it up and she just kept saying, "Don't stop, Don't stop!"

Soon, Jay had put a condom on and started fucking Becky. She started giving me head. This dude's dick had to be every bit of 10 inches. He was smiling at me while he was fucking her because she was moaning and squirming. I told him to "Let's switch." He pulled off the condom and I put on a condom. She was so wet, I knew she was turned on by both of us and I was extremely turned on by him. I think my dick was so hard that it could have snapped.

I started smacking my dick against her pussy and saying things in her ear; things like, "You see these two big dicks? You like these big dicks don't you? You gone let us fuck whenever we want?" Every question I asked, she replied, "Yes!" She was sucking Jay's dick the entire time I was whispering in her ear. I got to see his dick up close and in person.

I started fucking her while she kept sucking Jay's dick and before long she was squirting. I had Jay saying, "Damn, nicca you made her squirt" and he was moaning like shit because she was deep throating his dick. Little did he know, she squirted quick and hard only because he was there. She had always squirted before but never like that. I was into it more than ever because he was there.

She became a regular to get beat-down with Jay and other boys to come. I never charged her for that service but I did receive some type of compensation. It was never more than a couple hundred bucks, for me it was just about having fun. I was not escorting at the time and I did this a lot. Through it all, I remained HIV Negative.

******

Felicia hooked me up with one of home girl's right after my 25th birthday in December of 2003. I had been saying for the past two years that I wanted a baby of my own. I had been raising the twins and I so wanted a child. Hell, I could afford it and was going to be the best dad ever. I just needed a surrogate that would carry my child. I was willing to have sex with a woman or do artificial insemination if I had to. At the time artificial insemination would cost about $10,000.00 after the insurance from my job kicked in. I could surely afford that so I was on the search looking a great prospect. I was telling all my friends and I even offered to pay the person who carried my child and would allow them to have a relationship with my child. I was going to keep my baby and raise it alone. I knew that no one could love my child and give my child everything they would need besides me.

The first woman to step up to the plate was September, she was Felicia's friend and coworker at the bank. September was very nice, had a job, she wanted a baby and she was a lesbian with a girlfriend. The only problem was she wanted joint custody and she kind of looked like a man. Well hell, she was a man just in a woman's body. She dressed like a man, acted like a man and even had a damn beard.

I was skeptical because my child would be confused more than I was as a teenager about my mother and her lesbian relationships, but I was desperate, so I was down. She wanted to actually have sex and have her girlfriend there to watch us. I was fine with that but I knew I needed to get fucked up first, I mean really fucked up to do this. She was not my type by far. Man or woman, she was just not what I would want to fuck even for money but she was cool as hell so we set it up.

We made it through the New Year of 2004 and celebrated at Felicia's house. Everyone was there. It was the party crew like always with extra friends and family members. It was the best brining in 2004. I had too much to be thankful for. All I needed to make my life complete was my baby. While everyone was getting messed up; Felicia, September, her girlfriend and I slipped into Felicia's room. We talked about how we'd handle this situation and I had to admit to them that I was nervous.

I'd never had sex with a lesbian. I didn't want to say that it was the fact that the lesbian looked like a man so I kept that part to myself. It kind of turned me off, but all I could think of was having a baby and I wanted that over everything else. After our little discussion September and her girlfriend followed me home. We were well on our way to make our baby. Crazy, because the entire twenty minute ride to my house I was thinking of baby names, what my baby was going to look like, and what the sex would be. I was thinking if it was a boy, I was going to have to learn sports and that manly shit and if it was a girl, hell I was good!

Once we arrived at my house, we went into my bedroom. Nina was gone with her baby daddy and had the kids with her. We were all home alone. I turned the radio on and was certain to turn off every light in the house! I wanted it pitch black so I could think of someone else. However, September's girlfriend wanted to see everything. She got to saying how she didn't want me to touch all over September and no kissing and no this and that.

I was just about ready to tell that bitch to the shut the fuck up right before September did. I was glad she stepped up, because if not, her girl was going to have to leave. She was already spoiling a mood that I really wasn't in to begin with. They went to the bathroom and I started jacking off. They came back out the bathroom and they both were naked. I was thinking, "What the fuck!" However, not to spoil what was going on, I kept jacking my dick.

They both lay on my bed next to me and started rubbing, kissing and September was eating her girlfriend out. I was watching them while slowly stroking my dick. It was kind of interesting because I had never watched two black women have sex. It was way different than white women. September and her girlfriend were more intimate and I liked it. My dick was harder than a dogs bone, I was ready to fuck. That thought was ruined when September's girlfriend burst out, "Don't stick your dick in her until you are about to bust." I stood behind September while she was eating her girl out. I really wanted to smash but I was like, "Okay!"

I lost my erection because it was just too many damn stipulations and the mood had been ruined. I told them I had to go into the bathroom to jack off and I would be back. My dick was now softer than a boiled spaghetti string and to top it off, I couldn't get hard again. I had to come out and tell them that we needed to set up for another time. They were cool with it, we all got dressed and they left.

The next day Felicia informed me that September had told her that she didn't want to do it anymore and would rather do the insemination, but I would have to pay for everything. I was like 'Fuck no!" That bitch had a job just like me and made more than me. She wanted joint custody so I wasn't paying for nothing in full if I couldn't keep my baby, so we never finished what we had started and I was fine with that. I didn't want a woman that looked like a man to be my kid's mother anyway. It would've been nice, but not worth it in the end.

Next person on the list was Lillianna, we called her Lilly for short. We worked for the same credit union but she worked at a different branch; she was cool as ever. Lilly was a white girl who acted black, attractive with curves and a great breasts. I really liked her because she loved the fact that I was honest with her about everything. She already had kids and didn't mind carrying mine. She was attracted to me, liked me and I liked her, so it was easy to do what we needed to. However, she had a boyfriend and her tubes were tied.

Her boyfriend was a member of the credit union and I saw him regularly because he used my branch. After many conversations, he finally came around to the idea. I offered to pay for the surgery to have her tubes untied and for the process of insemination. The entire process was right under $20,000.00! I wanted a kid bad as hell; I had the money so I was like, "Let's do this shit!" Lilly was beautiful with flawless hair and her children were even more beautiful. I knew my child was going to be the bomb with our genes united.

Candy was my cute home girl and we worked together at the credit union. The more I thought about the surgical cost of having a child with Lilly the more Candy began to feel like a better option. We hung out an entire year before we decided to have a child. Candy knew about my past ideas of having a child with two different women. She was already a great foster mother to two of her cousin's children. She wanted joint custody but was cool with the fact that my kid was going to live with me. We talked about sex and insemination but decided to cross that bridge once we got to it.

Candy had a boyfriend who was in and out of jail and she loved him, wanted a baby too so we ran into a roadblock, I had to lay it out for her though. I told her that we needed to talk, I knew she loved to eat, so we went out to Red Lobster. Over drinks I sparked up the conversation telling her all the facts and left the decision up to her. I suggested she sleep on it over night because we had to get the ball rolling. It was the end of February and if we started now, my child would be here by my birthday.

I let Candy know that the other person that wanted a baby with her didn't even have his shit together, so we're going to start off by saying you would be a single mom with a dead beat baby daddy to begin with not to mention he's a convicted felon with no job, no crib, no car, no money and nothing else that matters to get ahead in life. To make matters worse he's still fucking his ex-girlfriend every time he gets out of jail. He's just not the right person to be a dad. I told her that those were all the facts.

The next morning while riding to work, Candy called me and said "Let's make this happen; I'm ready!" I was happy as hell. I just needed to know which way we were about to roll, were we going to be having sex or insemination? I was anxious while riding in to work. Once there we began our day on the Teller line as usual. We sat right next to each other and talked the whole day about having our baby.

Candy wanted joint custody. My child would live with me during the school year and with her in the summer. She wanted to be in my child's life fully and I didn't have a problem with that. I wanted my child to know its mother, but I would be the sole provider. I liked her because we were so open and honest with each other and close; I thought. Only time would later tell that, that wasn't the case.

After work we had a long conversation about our child (yes our child), we decided on artificial insemination. Because of our relationship, we both felt we didn't want to cross those lines. I was cool with that, and I offered to pay for the process. We scheduled our first doctor's appointment at the clinic for the procedure in Minneapolis. We were told how the process went and the exact cost after insurance. We were finally about to start the process to have a kid and it would be here by February or March of 2005!

I was going to have to jack off into a cup, while Candy would have to have others things done. We started the process in the beginning of April. Candy went along with me to all my appointments. She sat in the waiting area while I did what I had to do in the back room. It wasn't that bad at all, it was just like I'd seen on TV. There was a small room with a TV, VCR, magazines and lube. I could have brought anything I needed and Candy could have come in the room if I needed her too.

I didn't have to bring any magazines nor did I need Candy present, I had enough images in my mind to leave a specimen. Once finished, I placed the cup in the window and we left. They needed to examine my sperm and Candy insisted that we take an HIV test as well because of my lifestyle. Hell, I wanted her to take one because of her boyfriend being in and out of jail. I always said, "He isn't going back for crimes, he has a man in there!" We always laughed but I was serious, this dude would get out and go right back every single time, as a matter of fact he's there right now.

Once the results came back NEGATIVE and all testing of my sperm turned out good, it was time to start the insemination process. A couple of days before our VERY IMPORTANT appointment, Candy dropped a bomb on me. She said she had been having sex with a dude named ElShanti Hunter! Not only had they been having sex, they had unprotected sex! I was pissed to the max for two reasons; first, they'd had unprotected sex, and second she knew I was fucking with him too!

I was fucking with ElShanti while she was fucking him. I was fucking him first, and she knew I pulled him first! Who the fuck does some shit like that? "Candy, that's who!" I was beyond pissed. She said he had been coming on to her and she gave in. Needless to say, we called off the baby idea, and I severed our friendship. That was some real foul shit. I lost a good friend in her and lost a good fuck buddy in him. I was livid so, I told everyone that I was fucking Elshanti, and he had a mean ass curve to his cut dick, with some low hanging balls. I felt like he took my baby, so I wanted to take his reputation. No More Baby!

CHAPTER 11

THE TRIP TO MINNESOTA

A fter all I had been through I finally feel like I'd made it. The long battle with trying to get my mother and father to really accept me and my lifestyle and my illness, I thought we've finally reached the point that I was yearning for.

I went back to Minneapolis from Atlanta once again to see everyone and reconcile any differences that were out there. My first stop was through Indianapolis where I visited my cousin Antawyone who's my Uncle Kenny's son. I visited for a couple of hours, we chatted and some of his friends even purchased my book while I talked about it with them. The support had already started and that was just my first pit stop.

I was on the road to Chicago and arrived about 4am where I checked my Face Book and Twitter and crashed laying down talking next to Lucciano. I love that kid because I had seen so much of myself within him. I motivated him to better himself and he inspired me never to look back.

I was on my way to Minneapolis the very next morning only having about five hours of sleep. I never stopped in Gary, Indiana because it was dark and too late. **Real Hard Blank Stare** I touched down in Minneapolis and went straight to Timothy's house about 6pm. He was a new found best friend that moved to Minnesota from Atlanta the year I moved out of Minnesota to Dallas, Texas. He was also the best friend of my cousin Felicia's friend Debra; small world.

I showered, changed clothes, went to Pepito's, grabbed three enchiladas for myself and a burrito for cousin Kim. Then on the way to Felicia's house, I sang my heart out for Timothy, he recorded it and posted it to Face Book. I sang a total of three songs before I eventually became hoarse. The highway had won and took my voice away. I sang Jennifer Hudson's song "Gone" and I had dedicated it to #26.

It seemed like I had known Timothy forever. We chatted just about every day now and he was helping me in more ways than one. Once we arrived at my cousin Felicia's house, Fatboy and Boo, Fatboy's oldest son was waiting for me and Felicia, Delores and Kim came back from picking up Bre; Felicia's daughter from work. Afterwards we all sat around and had the famous round table discussion. My friend Molly came, then my cousin Nikki and her wife Keysha and Keysha's children. Yes, I said her wife and children! My cousin had just gotten married a couple of months earlier in Markham, Illinois. It felt so good to be surrounded by family and friends and I could just totally be myself. I was always myself around them.

The next morning I didn't want to get out of bed because I had a stomach ache from eating three enchiladas with sour cream, extra cheese, guacamole, and heavy sauce the night before, which I'd been craving for months. I finally got out of bed, showered and began my journey of dropping off books. I stayed a while having small chat with a few customers about the book while others I took pictures with, like Lisa and Regina. Regina worked as a nurse at Abbot Clinic in Minneapolis.

I went to the Credit Union, my former employer and spoke with the Branch Manager who was my former supervisor and coworkers. I also had the chance to see a member whom I looked up to as a grandmother figure. She purchased two books and we exchanged contact information. I left out of the Credit Union having sold a total of ten books and gaining their support.

Then I met back up with my new found bestie Timothy. We were both starving so we did a couple of errands before hitting up The Best Steak house on Nicolet Ave. I got my fat boy grub on. I ordered the lunch special which was an 8 oz. sirloin steak, baked potato with extra sour cream and extra butter, butter grilled toast and a salad. I contemplated ordering dessert but didn't want to have another episode of this morning from over eating.

After dinner Timothy rode with me to grandma's house. On the way we sang songs by Mary J. Blige and talked about men we'd encountered. We shared lessons of do's and don'ts, what we did and how we both got out the previous situation. Before long we arrived at my grandmother's house and from there we hit up Nikki's, Kiwana's, Kenny's, my mother & brother's house. My mother had moved in with my brother Romie and his wife Tonya. She explained that her neighbors were running a drug lab in the apartment above hers and she didn't feel comfortable living there anymore.

My mother was talking to me like she was crazy but not in a disrespectful way, at first. I knew that she was trying to be sarcastic because she eventually made the statement, "It was very disrespectful of you to write about me in your book now people want to kill me, I've lost friends and now my grandchildren don't even want to talk to me." She stated that I could have told what was going on within my own life and left her life out of it and that she had considered even filling a lawsuit. She then said I was a disrespectful ass child!

I told her that the book was not about her but it was about what had happened to me and because she played a major part in what happened in my life, that's why she was included. She proceeded to tell me again that I was disrespectful and GOD don't like ugly and I was going to pay for what I had done. I tried to give her a hug and she resisted and said, "No." After that, I left out of her room and went into my brother's room because at that point I felt like crying but I was not about to give in to her shenanigans and she was not about to ruin my trip. I hadn't driven nearly 19 hours to feel bad so on that note, I left her where she stood.

My little niece Zadie who's is named after my mother, kept saying she wanted to come live with me once I went into my brother's bedroom. I asked Tonya, how things were now that my mother is living there with them? She said, "I have no comment," with a very hard side stare!

I told my niece that if it was okay with her mom and dad that of course she could come and stay with me. She said, "I only want to stay for a little while, like three or four months." We all laughed and I told her that if she did, she would have to stay for the school year and go to school. She looked at me confused and looked at her mom and said, "Okay Uncle Sam."

I hugged Lil Zadie and kissed her forehead and told her that she's always welcome to come visit me anytime she liked. She and my brother walked with me outside to my car and I left. I wanted to take full advantage of the 4 days that I was to be in Minneapolis. I had to ensure that I saw everyone and did everything that I wanted to do before I headed back home to Atlanta.

That night, Timothy and I went to the "Gay 90's Club" which I hadn't been to in over 2 years since I left Minneapolis and it was a blast. I felt like a celebrity running into just about everyone that fucked my husband. **Blank Stare** They were all my so called friends and some I had even called my best friends at some point. There were about four or five guys all together but one person in particular stood out. His name is Marquise, he wears dreadlocks and seemed very scared upon noticing me however I didn't have an ounce of animosity towards him. After all, his loyalty was with my husband and not to me. I completely understood why he smiled in my face while living in Minnesota, he had to in order to keep fucking Price and getting it when he wanted it or whenever Price wanted it.

After a while, he approached me, gave me a hug, apologized and even offered to buy me a drink but I politely declined. I wasn't that forgiving but the gesture was more than nice. He explained how he too fell in love with Price and that they had a thing going on for over a year. WOW I was totally speechless, needless to say. I couldn't believe he even admitted that to me. He also stated that he had been visiting Price in Chicago and how Price paid for the hotel rooms but Marquise eventually broke it off with Price after finding out that Price was in a relationship with Arius. I had to tell him, "Price was in a relationship with a lot of people;" sexual relationship that is. Price didn't understand the word "monogamy."

After a couple of drinks and taking over the DJ booth, I had totally forgot about all the whores that I was surrounded by. I was at home and dared a bitch to step to my face. They wouldn't be able to walk away and Timothy and I were well prepared for anyone that felt "froggy."

Leaving the club, I felt on top of the world. Timothy snapped a couple of pictures of me in my "I love NYC" shirt and I knew I stood out. I felt even better turning heads and turning down men because I had a REAL MAN back in the A; #26. We went our separate ways until the next day.

The other reason that I was in Minnesota was to evict my tenant. DAMN, AGAIN!!! It was just the year before that I was evicting my previous tenant. She had three police calls which one of them was a drug call and per my lease and the City of Brooklyn Center, she had to be evicted unfortunately. To top it off, I knew that I had a mess on my hands because she was nasty as hell.

Upon entered the front door of my rental house I wondered how people live like this. But I had to keep in mind that some people are just not good tenants. Some homeowners don't want to rent out to Section 8 tenants because most of them live trifling. This woman had seven people living in a three bedroom house and didn't have the decency to take most of her stuff which she left behind for me to dispose of and clean after. I'd driven 19 hours to get there and had to spend a whole day cleaning the place and getting it ready for my new tenant.

Thank GOD for my new bestie Timothy and friend Delores, because we spent eight hours cleaning that house from top to bottom. I also had to hire a professional carpet cleaning company because she'd had a flood and didn't inform me nor my best friend Michelle who was the Property Manager. I also spent time on the phone with my insurance company. I accomplished a lot on that day yet found time to kick it with friends later that night.

The next day my new tenant moved in and I was back on the road headed home before noon. I stopped in Chicago because I was not about to drive straight through. I stopped at Lucciano's and arrived their around 6pm that evening. It was Chicago's Gay Pride and I wanted to hit up Jackson Park. All the gays were going to be there and I wanted to be in the mix, we had a blast. We went back to Lucciano's where I fell asleep immediately before 4am. I guess it was the Ciroc that Lucciano had bought. I think I'd had too much and still needed leave the next morning.

I awoke that next morning around 9am, showered and revived myself so I was ready to hit the road. I was going to go to Gary and deliver some books but my spirit directed me otherwise. I didn't feel safe about going into the Color Doors Projects to deliver books so I made a post to Face Book informing those who had reserved books that it would be best to just order from my website. I apologized in advance but my safety was more important, although I stopped in Gary to see my best friend Michial, Aunt Denise, Janice the neighbor that stayed by my dad Robert and I also visited my real father Pete.

My father Pete and I talked for over an hour. He gave me words of encouragement, told me that he accepts me no matter what although he didn't understand my lifestyle at first, but he had to realize that it was my life and I am the one who had to answer to GOD. He said that he would be there to support me in anyway. Those words never left my mind as I drove back down that long lonely highway to Atlanta for the remainder of the ten and a half hours. I loved my father for what he stood for and I really loved him for supporting me and letting me know that he had my back no matter what.

At the end of the day regardless of what anyone else says, I have been through the storm and back, I have met the devil, after the storm the sun will still shine through it all.

******

My ex #26 was offered a promotion back in NYC which he strongly fought for. He wanted it so badly that he could taste it and we made multiple trips to NYC from Atlanta before the offer was even given. He had a total of three interviews for a higher position with New York Police Department (NYPD). He decided to take the position as Detective, but the moment was bittersweet for me; I was now losing someone that I had given my heart to. He left on the date of my 4th wedding anniversary; August 4, 2012. I completely understand the cliché" people are brought into your life for a reason, a season or a lifetime." Whether he was a season or a lifetime, he definitely came for a reason. He was my potter sent to help mend my heart from the many shattered pieces caused by my undying love to Price. I had honestly come into the relationship with trust issues but he was able to help me regain trust. I was living in a fairytale relationship and I didn't want to be awaken from my dream.

#26 Offered to pay the fees for me to break my lease here in Atlanta but I just couldn't leave. I prayed for over a month in that #26 would get the job. Once it was offered I prayed again and GOD must have heard me. HE whispered, "Don't Move Yet My Child, Your Works In Atlanta Are Not Done." I started school that fall semester. My major was Business Administration and I was in the process of writing my second book.

******

My THIS and your THIS maybe different but we both have a THIS. We all are going through a THIS. But just know THIS; THIS Too Shall Pass. We just have to make sure that we praise and glorify HIS name after THIS. It only gets better after THIS. I will not allow my past to turn me around.

Two years ago I felt just like Job in the Bible. Everything that the devil stole, GOD has been giving me back 10 FOLD. He is not through with me yet. TRUST ME...Troubles don't last forever. "Weeping may endure for one night but JOY cometh in the morning." The things that happened are my Testimony and through it all, I KEPT MY FAITH AND STILL BELIEVED. Through it all I've endured. I never turned my back on GOD and GOD never left me, I simply gave in. I STILL BELIEVE!

CHAPTER 12

THE DL MEN IN THE HOOD

Most of the death threats, hate emails and posts that I received were from the family and friends of the men that I listed in "Eyes Without a Face" in the "DL Men" chapter. Ironically I didn't receive any threats from the men that were named in the book but from their loved ones who were mad because I'd exposed those men. Hell, how did they think I felt when their family members had *sex with me as child?* I totally understood how they could feel the way they did but did they understand how I felt? I had lived with this secret of being these bastards' sex object from childhood to well over 20 years. It was time for me to come clean and get this shit off my chest, I just wanted to be free.

I received threats through Facebook and from the auto reply from my website www.samuelholloway3.com. I was told never to show my face again in Gary, Indiana; or I would have to be ducking and dodging bullets, these people wanted me dead. I had threats from not only men but women too.

Some of the threats were from people who had heard their names were in the book but they really weren't. Someone had lied to them I guess to see if they had actually fucked me too. If I had forgotten to list anyone in the DL Men chapter in my first book, I was definitely going to make sure that I didn't miss them the second time around in the second book. **Blank Stare**

People were actually mad because I used real names; first, middle, last and nicknames. Damn right, I sure did! I would do it all over again too. I wasn't about to let their ass get away with a damn thing. I wanted to make sure everyone knew about them. Hell, I even gave free books away and purposely sent them to the projects in Gary to make sure they asses were found out, I didn't give a fuck!

I also wanted to make sure I made other people aware, because I didn't want anything to happen to those children living in the projects the way that things happened to me. THEY HAD NOW BEEN WARNED! I was coming for everybody! I wasn't putting every man that I'd slept with in the book either. I was only placing the names of the men who molested me, or who had crossed me. If that were the case, I would be talking about men from almost every hood in Gary!

Again, the book wasn't supposed to be used as a blast book. It was to make others AWARE about what was taking place where they lived, or just give them insight on how DL Men live. Yes, I did also make sure that anyone who fucked me over to put their ass out there, but that was to make sure that they acknowledged their wrongs. I will not apologize for what I did or the way I did it, they never apologized to me. And, after I did it I felt much better and a weight had been lifted from my shoulders.

I had been thinking of my molesters and looking into their lives. Sadly, everyone had major issues. Some were dead, in jail or just not doing good at all. However, all of them had children. I thought to myself, "What if someone had done to their children, what they had done to me?" It bothered me because regardless of my feelings towards them, I still didn't want their children to suffer nor endure anything that I had. Their fathers used to fuck me like Interstate 94 going West and had no feelings behind it.

I started trying to take my power back. I didn't want their actions to hold me back any longer. First, I sought legal action. I had finally reported the crimes to Child Services who referred me to Adult Services because of my age. They in turn, gave me a detective's phone number located in Merrillville, Indiana. Before I called the detective, I finished my statement with Adult Services. I knew the "Statute of Limitation" had expired, I was making sure to dot all the I's and cross the T's. After giving my statement, I then called the detective back. I explained to her what had happened and told her that I had written a book with all of the guys that molested me real names within it. She told me that was one way of getting the word out about them. The detective then asked me for all of their names, ages, date of births and if I had any current or last known addresses. I gave her everything I knew about the men. She was going to cross check their names in the data base to check to see if any of them had a past record for molestation.

Some people say that I was looking for an apology. I kinda was, but more so I was looking for answers. I wanted to know why they did what they had done to me. I knew that was farfetched, but I still wanted to know. Out of all the men listed from Maurice "Munk" Moody, Antoine "Coop" Cooper, Michael Moore, Alex McKenney, Gregory "Double G" Conwell, Stacy Ray Whitt, and Anthony MaGhee I had direct contact with only one of them. I had become friends with Maurice on Facebook. Although he was in jail he managed to inbox me his phone number. Just like a criminal, this guy had a cell phone illegally in jail.

I called Maurice immediately after receiving his phone number. We talked about everything from back in the day including us having sex. I was in awe after he told me just about every encounter we had, some of which I had totally forgotten about. I couldn't believe how sexual I was as a young teen. This dude had been fucking me for years and not to mention, raw. He said he loved every time he came inside of me, which was every time we had sex, we never used a condom. To my surprise he said he was in my book! My mouth literally hit the floor as I dropped the phone. I was thinking, "Who told him?"

Maurice broke the news to me before I even told him that he was in the book. Immediately after my mind settled from the discourse that his response took me on, I wondered to myself, how did he find out? He stated that he had been in prison for the past 12 years. Maurice said that, "Your cousin who's locked up with me said my name is in your book." At that point I sensed that our nice conversation was about to go left field. He surprised me so much that I actually began to think about our past and be happy about it.

I did love him. I loved all of them. It wasn't the type of love that I experienced with Price, #26, nor Adonis, this was a different type of love that I really couldn't explain. It was right then and there that Maurice said those words that I had been waiting to hear from all of the men. "I'm sorry bro!" I became speechless as the tears rolled down my face. He continued to explain his actions. He stated that he was young himself and didn't know the effects that, that would have on me.

Maurice told me that he's always loved me. He said I was the first guy that he'd ever had sex with. However, he then went on to say if he could take it back that he wouldn't. He said he didn't regret it because he liked it. He liked taking care of me and making sure I was okay. He said he loved every moment that we spent together. I couldn't be mad because I understood how he felt. When we were together, his actions were just what he had said, he was very nice towards me but just always had rough sex with me.

Maurice and I had sex so many times that I lost count. He brought back memories of us having sex outside. Yes outside: We had sex next to an abandoned warehouse beside the train tracks behind DuSable Arms Projects, we had sex on the playground in the swings where I rode him, we had sex at a school in the open field, hell, we even had sex in a damn tree-house. I felt like a slut after we went through all of our sexual escapades, I was too damn freaky as a child.

I remembered calling him at times asking for sex. I would walk long distances at times to be with him. When he got his car he would come and pick me up. The older he got, the more mature he became. The last couple of times we had sex, Maurice had gotten us a hotel room, I felt special. We stayed at the Buckingham Motel off 22nd and Broadway. Looking back now, there was no reason at all to feel special. I should have felt nasty if I'd known better. That was a Motel for prostitutes but I guess that's all I was to him.

Looking back, Maurice had some good sex and a pretty dick. He was caramel, actually the same complexion as my husband, and "Double G." Red and yellow bones are my weakness and I see why now, they were all fine. Maurice's dick is straight, cut, shaved low hanging balls and was every bit of 8 to 9 inches. After our conversation, he gave me his address so I could send him a copy of my book.

Maurice also sent me some recent pictures of him shirtless in jail. I personalized his autographed copy by writing, "To Munk/ Maurice, the first guy that I gave myself to at an early age. I really can't express how I feel because my feelings are mixed. Thank you for that convo thou! I really needed that. Sam A.K.A. Robert." I really hope he understood his role in the book now that he has five children.

Right before Maurice had called me, I reached out to Antoine "Coop" Cooper. I loved him too. He had a very dark skinned "midnight" complexion. He was bowlegged, slightly hairy but mostly smooth skinned. He had white teeth, always kept a low cut fade and was always nice to me. He's currently serving a "Natural Life Sentence" in prison. This dude was actually crazy back then because he raped several women and even murdered some of them. The last time that we were together he told me that he had murdered a woman but I didn't believe him.

I found out which prison he was in and mailed him a copy of my book. I wrote a little note on the front cover. It read, "To Coop, my molester. My child hood lover. Looking back to when I performed those acts on you and your friends/brother, did you realize I was a kid?! Anyways, I loved you and I was not at legal age of consent. Here's to you, Shine bright like a diamond. Robert/Sam." I felt a little better after I mailed it and knew he received it because I sent it via Priority Mail with tracking. I was trying to take back my power, any little thing was going to help me do that.

Coop had slept with so many women and had children. He was sexy as ever to be chocolate. I didn't like chocolate men, but every time I thought of him, I got a little excited. He was the shit all the way around. I loved his body scent. I loved all of their body scents. I grew to love them after the many sexual encounters we had, but I loved Coop's dick a lot because it was pretty. The majority of them had pretty dicks. Coop's was long, thick and slightly curved but straight. It was circumcised with a nice fat head and low hanging hairy balls. I had Coop so many times that I can't count them, let alone remember every encounter.

Michael Moore, Coop's younger brother who died from "Cirrhosis" a few years before my book was published, had a couple encounters with me. We first started off at my house from him coming to see if my brother was at home one day and I gave him head. He must've really liked it because he returned again later that night along with his friend Stacy and it happened all over again with both boys. Next time was at his house across the street. I never got the chance to say anything to him before he passed away. Some days later I felt an urge to suck his dick again and before I knew it, I was. I believe I was building an addiction for these young men. As a child, I didn't know then that what I did was wrong since no one ever took the time to tell me otherwise. So I was doing what I thought was right because I thought they liked and loved me the same way I loved them. Once inside the house we went into the kitchen. His dick was rock hard and long. He told me to get on my knees and open my mouth. He held his hands on the door frame above his head swinging back and forth while his dick was in my mouth fucking my throat. I will never ever forget the way he moaned the entire time.

He then stopped and told me to bend over while he tried pushing his wet dick into my dry ass. His dick was wet from me sucking on it. It was too big to into my 12 year old ass. He didn't use lubrication nor a condom. After that didn't work, he went back to fucking my throat until he came inside my mouth. Those were the only three times we had gotten together. His dick was actually a little bigger than his brother Coop and it was prettier too. Michael's complexion was the same as Alex and his dick was super thick, cut with a fat ass head and low hanging hairy balls.

Another one of the men that molested me from the hood was Alex who was killed in September of 2014. I felt bad because he was killed. I wouldn't wish that on my worst enemy. Soon after I had time to think, I had mixed emotions, part of me was upset because before he was killed, he disrespected my relationship with my husband. Not that any others hadn't done it before, but he did it so bluntly, he didn't give a fuck.

I had come to Gary to visit family and ran into my cousin Nikki and then girlfriend Keysha (now wife). Nikki told me that someone wanted to see me so come to her house. I had no idea who it was so I went but I must admit that I was both surprised and excited when Alex pulled up on a motorcycle because I hadn't seen him in a long time. He was beautiful, buff, had a banging body and still had those sexy muscular hairy legs. His voice was so deep. I honestly fell in love as soon as I saw him, but I remembered I was married and quickly shut out that thought of having him again.

He got off the bike and gave me a hug that I will never forget. He was so happy to see me. I started having instant flash backs of having his dick in my mouth at 12 years old. I was looking at him like, "Damn, I had that thug ass dude right there!" Alex started talking to my cousins, and I told Price who he was and all about our past history. I kept nothing from Price, although I should have because Price became instantly pissed off at hearing the details.

Alex asked me to come to the back of the car. Price was sitting in the back seat with the door open rolling a blunt. Alex then asked me to come to a hotel with him later. I told him that I was married and that that was my husband sitting right next to me listening to us. He blatantly said, "Okay, you still coming to the hotel later?" I looked at him in disbelief and said, "No, I'm good bro!" Now in my mind, I wanted to go bad as hell, I really wanted to go. Price and I were having our problems and were not having sex anyway. I figured Alex would do me just right at that time. But I respected my marriage and passed up some dick that I knew was going to be the best dick ever.

At 12 years old until around 14 years old, I was Alex's toy. He used to invite me over in the beginning to come play with his toys. It was never the toys that I played with. I would always end up playing with his dick instead. I was fine with that at 12 years old. I loved Alex. He was so nice to me before he found out about Munk and me. I remember most days going over his house after school. He stayed with his dad who seemed to never be at home, or he was always at work. Alex would have me sucked on his dick all the time to the point that I lost track. It felt like I was sucking his dick on a daily basis.

Alex would always try and push his dick as deep as he could down my throat. It was always hard for me to deep throat him, his dick was so big, it was every bit of 9 inches when I was 12. He was cut, thick with low hanging balls, with a slight mean curve to the right and his dick was on point. He had pretty feet too, his second toe was a little longer than the rest of his toes.

I learned that Greg "Double G" Conwell was married, still living in the hood on Kentucky Street along with his wife. His daughter must be in her 20's by now. I had only seen him once while visiting Gary in the summer of 2012. He didn't even speak to me, let alone even look at me. He paid me no attention and I did the same in return. There were no heart feelings at all. I loved him as a child and I loved his little, but big body. He was sexy as hell but rather little for his age.

The first time that we ever hooked up was in his car when he had me suck his dick while he was driving. Double "G" wanted to nut while we rode up Martin Luther King Jr. Drive and back. Of course, I accomplished that mission. After that, I would see him at night coming home and I would take out the trash so he could see me. The dumpster was the midpoint from my apartment to his apartment. He would see me taking out the trash just about every time he came home at night. I knew what I was doing. I wanted him bad as hell, since Coop was no longer around like that.

The next time we hooked up, he was coming home drunk and I was taking out the trash like usual. Double "G" got out the car and called me over and said to follow him but wait 20 seconds. He started running slowly into the bushes next to the abandoned building behind the projects. It was adjacent to the burned down "Good Corner." I waited the 20 seconds and began to follow behind him. He stopped next to the abandoned building and about the time I met up with him, he was already jacking his dick. He had his shorts down and his shirt over his head. It was the summer so the weather was just right.

Double "G" told me to suck his dick. His tone sounded sexy to me at that time. Looking back now, it was said very aggressively. I started sucking on his dick, and within minutes he had came. He always made sure I swallowed his nut by pushing my head down. I sucked his dick one more time, after that he cut me off. I had fallen in love with him and left a note in his mail box. It was very sexual and I told him how much I loved him. Funny thing was, I never put my name in the letter but he knew who had written it. I was 14 years old when I did that. He didn't come at me mad or angry. He was actually polite and just said that anyone could have read that letter but lucky he got it before someone else went into the mail box. I was honestly devastated because I loved him but I understood. He had a pretty dick like the rest too. It wasn't that big, but it was right for me. It was nice and cut and his balls were not as big as the rest. I loved his feet too, they were so cute and seemed well maintained.

Stacy Ray Whitt had pissed me off. He was on Face book and posting stats that he had written a book about his life and his struggles and promoting the fact that he was about to become a rapper. A rapper at 40 something and talking about his struggles? I was confused and pissed. I was wondering had he written in his new book about having a 12 year old boy sucking on his dick. So what I was thinking about his book spilled over onto his page and his actual post somehow. People started commenting on it and asking him if it was true. He immediately deleted my comment and blocked me. He never addressed me nor asked me anything. Right after that, his girlfriend of 17 years, Donita Smith began posting about me. She was saying all types of negative shit. That piss me off, and initiated a Facebook war.

This bitch had posted a status that read, "If all this shit happened you didn't tell anyone your brother, the police nobody a best friend, Wouldn't you want some type of Justice done!! But instead you trying to get paid!! Get the Hell out of here!! His moms boyfriend is the one he got molested by isn't that what he said in the book!! But yet you still focused on Stace!! Cmon naw!! Stacy has had too many women in his lifetime to even be thinking about a man!!"

That post set me off and I lost it and I went into a rage. How in the hell is this bitch going to tell me I'm lying? They weren't together when he did that. I didn't give a fuck if she even knew him at that time, it didn't matter to me. She didn't know what the fuck she was talking about and that's exactly what I told her. Eventually she would end up blocking me too. But not before she threatened me via face book by suing. I have yet to see a court date because of slander in my book. I would have thought that if Stacy felt I was lying, he would have sued immediately. But three years later, and still nothing! I can only say, he knows the truth and he was not about to open that can of worms!

However, Stacy had many children like some of the others. Some of his children were now grown and had learned of what was posted about their dad on Facebook. Some people were mad, telling me that his children could see it. My reply was, "Good, I don't give a fuck. I want them to see it! They have every right to see what type of monster their father really was!" In the end, I was a little happy because Stacy's sister who stayed behind us in the projects had in-boxed me on Face Book and confirmed that she had seen her brother a couple times leaving our house out the back door.

I believe that Stacy and I only had two encounters that I remember. The first was when he came along with Michael Moore and they had me sucking their dicks back to back while they sat on my mother's blue couch. The second time was when he had come back that same night after he and Michael had left and had me suck his dick alone. He came in my mouth both times. His dick was kind of musty, but it wasn't a bad musty smell that I could not stomach. I never saw his balls but his dick was extra-long and thick, was a bright complexion, cut and every bit of 10 inches.

Anthony MaGee was the one dude that I had that I didn't like out the entire crew. His dick stunk and he was uncut. He was not height and weight proportionate to me either. I was 14 years old now so I really knew what I wanted. He was kind of fat, however he was kind of attractive in the face. Today, he still lives in Gary, has children, served time in prison and was a complete alcoholic. There's nothing else to be said about him. I never saw him after he had fucked me and came inside of me and on my legs. His karma was already in rotation.

When some people tell me to stop speaking about these men because they have children, lives, wives, girlfriends and whatever else; I tend to think of this for myself. I am 35 years old. Those things that they had done to me started at 12 years old. Whether I wanted it or not, I was a child who could not consent. A child that didn't know what I was doing in the beginning was not right. At the end of the day, I can still smell them, feel their touch, and I can see clearer now more than ever of the things that we had done. I am a man who was a boy that now has a voice.

******

When I was 18 years old in the late summer of 1998, I lived in the Color Doors projects. It was late summer right before my deceased friend Keisha went to Indianapolis. Everyone was outside just like usual. All the hood boys and some hood boys from across the tracks and the girls too. There were a couple boys from 22nd also in "The Doors" nickname we called the projects. Moon had just finished doing my hair. I had some fingers waves that were in a high freeze, bitch, my hair was the shit.

Mikey D rode up on his bike talking shit. He was calling me fags and punks. I ignored him because I didn't want to get jumped. His brother Sean who is now deceased was there too. Mikey D was known for shooting people. I wasn't scared but I wasn't stupid either. My girl Keisha was like, "Robert, beat his mother fucking ass, he ain't nobody! I dare him to hit you because I'm gone whoop his ass!" Keisha was always down to protect me.

I just continued what I was doing which was talking to the girls and tried to ignore him. I was pissed because I did like him, and he could tell by the way I stared at him every time I saw him. We were all in my court, the projects were section off and wrapped around in a circle outlay. Mikey D would ride his bike by me and continue to call me names. Right when he started throwing rocks and sticks at me, my cousin Black Black stepped on the scene.

My cousin Black Black said, "Cousin, I know you not gone let this punk call you names and throw shit at you and you not gone do nothing?!" As soon as I saw my cousin, I went into fight mode. After he said that, Mikey D rode back up and said, "Yo fag", and before he could even get "get" out his mouth, I was on his ass. We were on the sidewalk and I grabbed him by his ponytail because he had long hair. I commenced to beating the shit out of him. I was hitting him in his head and face all while telling him, "You gone leave me the fuck alone, call me a faggot now bitch, you gone learn to respect me mother fucker!" I snapped out.

After a while of fighting on the sidewalk, we ended up in the grass. Then it happened. I fell and Mikey D fell on top of me. Keisha instantly hit and pushed him off me. When she did that, Sean hit me. My cousin hit him and said, "Ain't nobody bout to jump my cousin, y'all got me fucked up!" We both were now standing up and I went right back in giving him a couple more face shots before his brother broke us up. Black Black said, "I bet you won't fuck with him no more!" I was like, "I'll be right back bitch, let me go wrap my hair up!"

I had just gotten my hair done but we fell in the grass and dirt now my hair was all messed up. When I walked through the door of my apartment, my mother and dad Robert were there. My mom jumped up and asked what happened so I told her I had just got done fighting Mikey D. I guess she thought I lost because how my hair looked and I was dirty. She told me to come on because I was about to fight his ass again. I wrapped my hair up and walked back outside with my mom. I was following behind her and noticed she had a gun. Keisha was following behind me and my dad was behind her.

Mikey D was still standing out there after getting his ass kicked. My mom was snapping and was like, "Who the fuck is Mikey D" as we walked up. Somebody out there was like, "Him, that's Mikey D," and pointed to him. My mom was like, "Robert whip his ass and ain't nobody else gone touch my son!" I did what I did best. I began to whoop his as again. He didn't, well couldn't hit me, not one time. I had beaten the living shit out that boy. After I was done, I took my scarf off and said, "And bitch you fucked up my hair, I should beat your ass again!" But we all just walked back to the house. Some people called me messy before but that's what I call being messy.

Later on that year on December 12, 1998, my best friend Keisha passed away and a part of me died with her. I was extremely sad every day after that. Christmas slipped by and New Year's was right around the corner. Mikey D called me out of the blue one night, drunk, late as hell, and asked what I was doing and did I want some company. I was wondering how he even got my number. My mom was at work so I figured why not, I had no clue of what was about to go down but Mikey D was at my house within fifteen minutes. He took his shoes off at the door because of the snow and sat down on the couch reeking of alcohol.

We talked a while before he asked for some fellatio. That was not a problem because I'd wanted to do it for a minute now. He told me to "Get that dick," so I pulled down his pants and boxers. I didn't have to pull his pants down much because he was always sagging. I then spread his legs after I took one leg out of his pants. He had a very pretty nice "Little Dick." I gave him head until he came and he wasn't a minute man either, just a little man. After I was done he went to sleep right where he was. I let him sleep until just before 7am and told him he had to go before my mom came home. The next day, I told everybody because I knew he wasn't going to beat my ass and because he had been fucking with me for being gay and there he was; being gay!

CHAPTER 13

YOU CAN'T STEAL MY JOY

Just when I thought things had changed within my family, the more I realized things were the same. I was admitted into the hospital in April of 2013. This was my fifth time going into the hospital, the wire holding my teeth together from the carjacking had now infected my gums on both sides of mouth although, the wire was located on the bottom front of my mouth. So now my body was fighting two diseases; HIV, and a full mouth infection (Osseous). Unfortunately individuals who are HIV positive tend to have issues with T Cells trying to balance themselves to maintain good health. When other illnesses like PTSD, Depression and Osseous comes into the picture the T Cell count goes down which is a recipe for disaster. My T Cell count dropped drastically from 1100 to 405, but I was still "Undetectable" by the last time I had entered the hospital. If that wasn't enough of stress with no pain, I was told that I could possible expire within six months to a year. *DIE!* That's what the doctor and nurses were telling me. I needed surgery, and I needed a surgery ASAP!

Unfortunately, my insurance did not cover oral surgery. I was a damn wreck. Funny thing is, all I could think of after hearing the news was, "Who was going to take care of Tabby?" I didn't have the funds to pay for a surgery. I didn't have a job but I still had my property and other means of income. My best friend Timothy through his research found a great Oral Surgeon who would do the surgery. I started calling family and friends and informed them of my situation. Following my sister Teresa's recommendation I opened up a Charity Account at Wells Fargo Bank where family and friends could make donations to help me pay for my surgery.

I felt very low because I was always able to provide my own means. For a moment I had a flashback and realized how I could create the money I needed. I wanted to get out there and sell my body. I only needed $4000.00. I could make that in one night with the connects I had if I wanted too. I had new connects that I had never used and they had been begging for a night of lust. Being that, that was my past, I had never acted on it, but I sure as hell wanted to now. I had to be honest with myself. Everyone knew my status and they still didn't care. But that was not the road I was taking, I knew where I had been and I know where I was going.

This is when I found out that there were three types of people in my life: the people who helped me in my difficult times, the people who left me in my difficult times, and those who put me in my difficult times, ironically the people that stood by me were much unexpected. My sister immediately deposited some money into the account. Then it was my friends that I had just met not more than 2 years ago. Timothy was a major help in collecting money from our friends. I had some family members that I had not spoken to in years and some that I'd just met deposit money after Teresa and Tim had posted the news on Facebook, with my permission. If that wasn't surprising enough, a couple of my Professors from college had deposited some money too.

My mother, of all people turned her back against me, and had the audacity to send me a text message stating that if I would allow her to move in with me, that would be the *ONLY* way that she would help me financially. REALLY?! I thought. Your baby, your child, your seed, is faced with death, and you send me an ultimatum? I was too damn through and immediately cut her off. That was the very last string for me, I couldn't take her abuse any more. Going forward, I would have to learn how to love my mother from a distance.

If I that wasn't bad enough, my cousin Kyarra, posted on Facebook that I was dying, had six weeks to live, and was dying from having AIDS. This was the same person who had a baby with her own brother. My two cousins were having sex with each other. My Uncle Kenny's children that both have the same mother and father had now had a baby together. Did this bitch just throw a stone when she is living in a glass house? *YES, SHE DID!* Hello Pot, my name is Kettle; nice to meet you! **Side Stare**

So of course, being me, I replied and blasted her ass. I told her, "This ain't what you want love!" Since she had put my HIV status out there, well AIDS status as she thought and called it, I thought I'd make her feel what she thought she was trying to make me feel. The difference was, I had been living with my status for some time and I was 34, she had just started her journey and she was only 21. I told her that she was going to feel my wrath for some time to come, and I promised her that when I was done, she will break down and cry and wish like hell that she never knew me or fucked with me. And sure enough, when I was through, that bitch had called everyone saying that I was so wrong for doing that to her.

Her sister Nina, had forewarned her when Kyarra called her telling her what she was about to post on Face Book about me. My mother had gone over to Kyarra's mom's house, and told them that I had talked about them in my book "Eyes Without a Face" and that the book was about them. Nina told her that was a lie and that she should call me to ask. Kyarra went with that lie instead of asking the source. After all that, she tagged her brother's wife and his first baby's mother in the post. Kyarra also called them and said that I'd been talking about them in our Face Book thread. I hadn't said such a thing, I just told the truth; she had, had a baby with a man who was also her best friend's two babies daddy, who fathered two with his wife, and Kyarra's child was conceived in the middle of all the others. My cousin's wife bought into Kyarra's lie, that I was talking about her, so she called and cursed me out. I just let her talk and when she was done she hung up. I didn't even feel like arguing because it wasn't worth my time. I know what I said in my post was simply the truth.

Kyarra's other brother purchased two copies of my book. I never mentioned her, her mother or siblings, in my book. It had nothing to do with them but she believed my mother anyway and posted that bullshit on Facebook and of course, I had to cut her off after that. My mother had gone around telling family and friends that I had AIDS and was dying. I had lost weight due to being on a liquid diet because of the wire in my mouth and that crushed my spirit. I felt that my mother had a knife in my back and now she was just twisting it.

I did understand Kyarra's traumatic experience because she conceived a child and we both experienced incest. Hers was with her brother, and mine were with two of my cousins. When my other cousins read the book, they all thought it was one of my aunts or uncle's children. Some of my cousins were asking their siblings if they were mentioned in the book. I had to clarify for everyone that none of them are in the book. I then told them who the people mentioned in the book actually are which put them at ease from thinking it was whom they inquired about.

One lived in Memphis and he was my country cousin. He was now married with two children. I had last spoken to him when I moved to California. My mother had given me his number but I didn't even tell her it was him and I hadn't told anyone at that point. I was in total awe when my mother called me and gave me his number. As soon as we hung up the phone I called him and put the phone on speaker at my sister Lashenia's house so she could witness the call. This mother fucker hadn't changed one bit.

The conversation was good until he started reminiscing about what he had done to me and wanted me to visit him. I immediately ended that call and my sister was furious. The other cousin I had no clue of his whereabouts and I honestly didn't care. Both of them were around my brother's age.

Kyarra's older brother Kris and I, had a Twitter war. I had posted during Black History Month, that Martin Luther King would've wanted equal rights for everyone including Gay people. Kris then went on a rant on my Twitter wall saying, "That is a lie, I need to do my research and nobody cares about Gays!" That set me off. After going back and forth with a mutual friend of ours on Facebook, I told her that Kris must be Gay because he so worried about my life when he has hella Gay friends on his friends list.

Why is my gayness so important to him anyway? I wonder if he's straddling the fence himself. Hell, he even has a Gay brother and had two Gay uncles of which one is deceased. He could be "In the Closet Gay" and mad because I am living the life that he wants to live. With so many Gay family members close to him why are my choices such a problem in his life? Just like his sister, I had to cut him off after that episode because negativity is too damn draining and I have no room in my life for that foolishness.

I believe all of their animosity stemmed from the fact that I sued their mother back in 2002 for Identity Theft. Their mother was a Real Estate Agent who found me a house in Bloomington, Minnesota which I was about to purchase, but it needed too much work furthermore my Section 8 Tenant was given a specific move-in date and giving the condition of the house, her deadline could not be met. To add insult to injury the return on my investment was not lucrative either.

A couple of months later, I found out that my name was on the mortgage when I received a statement from the bank. I hadn't signed any paper work to purchase the home so I filed a lawsuit for Identity Theft. I took their mother to court and won. Those records are public so if they didn't believe the reason why I had sued her, they could look it up for themselves. Instead, she filled their heads with lies turning them against me.

I won a Civil Suit against her for $5,000.00, but I dropped the part where she had to pay me. It was not about the money for me, I just wanted my name clear. Since the lawsuit my relationships with two of her four children were severed. At the end of the day, I will always love my cousins but they would have to learn to respect me. They don't have to accept the fact that I am gay, but I commanded their respect going forward.

******

I eventually raised the money that I needed for my surgery. After the donations, I was just short of $2,000.00, but #26 came right on through and wrote me a check for the remainder and some. I knew that was nothing but the grace of GOD. He didn't bring me this far to leave me. I was set to have my first consultation and July 8th could not have come soon enough. I was nervous the entire drive to Augusta, Georgia. My bestie TaQuan whom I met through Timothy rode with me to my appointment. My friends had all talked about their schedule to see who could drive down with me for support.

TaQuan's schedule fit perfectly for the consultation. My appointment was scheduled for 8:30 am. TaQuan met me at my house and we pulled out at 6 am to allow ample time for us to get there. The trip didn't even feel like a two hour drive because we talked the entire way. It felt good to have people in my corner in my time of need. We arrived at the Georgia Regents University Augusta School of Dental Medicine without delay. TaQuan and I sat in the waiting room until they called my name. We watched "The View." I felt so comfortable. I was just eager to have the surgery to hurry and get past this horrible part of my life. I was going to be a new person with my braces having my full smile back instead of the partial fake one I had become accustomed to.

The nurse called my name finally but it really wasn't a long wait at all. I was very anxious to find out what needed to be done and how fast they could do it. Once I finally sat in the surgical chair, a doctor and a resident student looked in my mouth and charted there findings. They asked all types of questions from my medical history, family history to my HIV status. I had no problems telling them everything. The best part was when the doctor said the surgery would take about three hours total and could be set for next month August. I was elated that they were going to do the surgery, I didn't care how long it would take, I just wanted it done. Shit, that dentist could have said it was going to take 24 hours and I still would have been okay with that.

August 1, 2013 came faster than the speed of light. My surgery started at 10:30am. Quinton who's Kevin's boyfriend rode with me up to Augusta for the surgery. I picked him up around 8 am. We'd never ran into traffic issues driving to Augusta. However on that day we were delayed by traffic resulting from a car accident. We were only 30 minutes away before the huge back up. The traffic was gridlocked and I was nervous as hell because I didn't want to be late and have to reschedule the surgery.

I called the dental office and told the receptionist about the accident and that I was going to be late. She told me in return that, that would be fine because actually the doctor that was performing my surgery was stuck in the same traffic jam. I knew that, that was only GOD. Within a few minutes the traffic began crawling at a snail's pace but it was moving. We finally arrived there about 11ish. As soon as I was checked in, the nurse ushered me straight to the back, asked me a few questions and then put me under. I remember the doctor telling me to count backwards from 10 to 0. The only thing I remember was saying 10, 9, 8 and I was out.

When I had awakened, I was so damn high I could barely walk let alone talk. The nurses brought me outside in a wheel chair to the Outpatient pick up where Quinton was parked and waiting for me. On the ride home, the pain kicked in and to describe it would be as awful as the time I was pistol whipped nearly to death. I cried and held my mouth at the same time. We had to stop at Walgreens on the way back to get my Vicodin (pain meds). After leaving Walgreens, Quinton stayed with me at home until Kevin picked him up later. I was knocked out for the rest of the day. For the next couple of days I experienced pains that I would never wish on anyone. I was told by the doctor that I would be placed back on a liquid diet for the next four to six weeks because eating could cause an infection. I was so over the damn liquid diets, but I had to do it.

******

We all know my cycle — something good is followed by something bad. I was going through family issues, health issues, and now this publisher bullshit. That bastard still hadn't given me my money. He was running around like he was broke but he had no problem participating in Oprah's OWN Network's segment "Where Are They Now" (past celebrities). I know he got paid and still hadn't given me a damn dime! Fucking bastard!

I filed an order in the Civil Court to garnish his Chase Bank Checking account. Nothing! Then I went back and filed a Writ of Ficasi (Lien against a vehicle). This motherfucker already had a Title Maxx loan out on his 2002 Mercedes Benz Coupe from April of 2010 and still hadn't paid it off, so I was forced on as the second lien holder, which was fine by me, because it meant that he couldn't do anything without me getting something from that car if he sold or damaged it.

******

I had so much on my mind and was still going through a lot but I will never complain. I knew that if GOD had brought me to it, he sure was going to bring me through it. I also had to keep in my mind that the word through have the word rough in it, and I was going to eventually make it through this rough time. I was now becoming wiser. Everything was happening for a reason.

I was still dealing with Victim's Crime Compensation in Texas for the wire in my mouth trying to get them to pay for my surgery and braces. My court case was fast approaching; I'd eventually ended up suing my publisher for Breach of Contract. I was going through a lot with the person that had previously edited *Eyes Without A Face* because she wanted 25% from the sales of my books and to make matters even worse, I received several death threats after my first book was released and I had to move because my address was shared on Facebook.

Victim's Crime had initially started paying some of my dental bills and had paid all of my hospital bills. I was so thankful because just the hospital bills alone were over $10,000. I was losing my mind because I just kept getting bills after bills in the mail and I had no insurance to cover it. Remember, I didn't work, my rental properties were my income and I was now self-employed.

When I first started going to the dentist I was paying out of pocket. At one point, I had spent well over $3,000 and I still had the wire in my mouth and no braces. Once they had approved the dental work, I started receiving some reimbursements, after a whole year had passed. Then abruptly, my claim was denied again. "Are you serious?!" I called and spoke with so many people only to be told that the teeth that were on my claim were not the teeth that I had been fighting for. Victims Crime's had tooth #8 listed and that was also on my receipt from the dentist in Dallas, Texas. They had the wrong tooth number.

Having a lack of knowledge about how teeth are numbered I didn't know that my claim was disputing an injury to tooth #8 only. I don't think I was fully aware of the entire claim and its process. My mind at the time of fighting, most likely only saw wire in the letter and I went straight off of that. How in the hell could a wire just be on one tooth and to top it off, it was the tooth on the top level of my mouth listed in their rebuttal.

I had to go back and forth before they denied the claim entirely. I had to start the process all over beginning with the dentist in Dallas, which had just been purchased by another dental company. The law stated that every dental clinic had to keep medical records of patients for 7 years but they had no record of me at all. This was truly the devil working and playing his games.

I went through all types of hoops but luckily I had kept every piece of paper that was given to me. I spoke with the new owner, receptionist, and provided them with a copy of the panoramic x-ray and receipt that I was given on November 3, 2010 when the wire was initially placed in my mouth. After that, the dental clinic emailed me a letter stating that it was an error indeed on their end for not keeping my records. The x-ray had shown where the wire was placed so that's how they knew the receipt was incorrect.

I then contacted my previous dentist in Minnesota and had them provide me an x-ray proving that my teeth were in perfect condition during my last dentist visit and a letter explaining the same. This was too damn much. I had the perfect set of teeth before I left Minnesota and this accident was caused from the robbery that occurred in Dallas but I had to plead my case.

After that, I had to contact the dentist here in Atlanta and they provided corroborating information. Everyone worked quickly to get me the information that I was requesting because it was time sensitive. I had 30 days to respond back to Victim's Crime or they were going to drop my case.

On July 10, 2012, I had a 9:30 am telephone conference call with Victim's Crime. I was ready for this call, it had been almost two years and I was still fighting to get them to cover my bill for my braces; some straight bullshit. The call lasted about an hour with the Attorney General of Texas, a lawyer and someone else in the background that was typing the phone conversation.

They asked me a variety of questions that I had already been asked a long time ago. This was the 3rd and final appeal before a decision could be made. I was asked what happened all over again in detail piece by piece. This was horrible because it brought back the memories that I was so ever trying to forget, but in actuality, I could never forget November 2, 2010 because it seemed to me like it just happened yesterday.

I cried and cried as I explained what happened again. I was set up by my husband's lover and two of his friends. They beat me with a pistol and other blunt objects and left me for dead. They pulled the trigger four times attempting to shoot me but it jammed. I was left with my teeth hanging out of my mouth, a broken finger, broken ribs and cuts and bruises from my head to my feet. The right side of my body was broken. They had just left me for dead but through it all, I survived.

They told me to take my time while I broke down telling what happened. I was reliving the whole scenario all over again. Every time I heard the gun pull, I yelled out, "OH LORD, he shot me! He shot me!" But I'm still here. I was going in and out of consciousness and I just started praying. I let them have their way with me because I was helpless in the back seat of my car. I didn't do much of anything to defend myself except one hit to the perpetrator.

After I was done explaining what happened, they told me that I would hear back from them within 8 to 10 weeks. Damn, that was a long time to have to wait for an answer when I had a police report on file.

On August 28, 2012, the very next day after court with my former publisher, I got a call from Victim's Crime. It was about 9 am and I was dead sleep but jumped up when I saw that (512) area code pop up on my Caller ID, It was Brianna from Victim's Crime. She stated that they needed just a little bit more information so they could make a decision. *What the hell more could you want?* I wondered in a fucking dead sleep daze. *I was waking up to this fuckery,* I thought. She said that I needed to contact the Orthodontist that I was seen by, and who was placing the braces in my mouth to ask them to provide Victim's Crime with a letter stating why I needed braces on both layers of my mouth and not just the bottom layer where the injury occurred.

I asked her, "Was that it?" She said, "Yes." The thought came to my mind right away, "Bitch, I was on a liquid diet for almost 9 months. My bite was not correct so I was eating a different way. I couldn't whiten my teeth anymore and I had been doing that twice a year since 2007. More importantly, this fucking wire was still in my damn mouth and I couldn't even smile the way I wanted to, and smiling was my life!" I was beyond irritated at Brianna and Victim's Crime period. I was so over their asses and their shenanigans. They were acting like the money was coming from their own damn pockets.

Immediately I got up, called the Orthodontist whom I was seen by and spoke with the Office Manager Samantha and told her my situation. She told me she remembered who I was because of my story and she would provide the letter I needed and fax it in right away. She said that they had the fax number for Victim's Crime Compensation on file for me already. What a relief! The next day I called back to the dentist office to see if Samantha had faxed the letter. When she answered the phone she assured me that she had typed the letter personally and faxed it yesterday.

I then called Brianna at Victim's Crime but she didn't answer her phone. Go figure. I left her a voicemail and told her to call me back at her earliest convenience. She called back the very next day and said that she had received the fax and now they just needed to review it before a final decision could be rendered.

It took approximately six months for Victims Crime Compensation to tell me that they were denying any further claims and that the case was now dismissed and closed. I was pissed to the max. There I was left with a $3,500.00 out of pocket dental bill for my braces. I had inherited a $3,500.00 dental bill, and this wasn't even my fault. However, I had to look on the brighter side and not be angry. All my hospital bills had been paid along with the dental work finished previous to surgery, and I was reimbursed for some of the dental work that I had already received so ultimately, I was blessed.

*****

I was scheduled for court with my lawsuit against the publisher on August 27, 2012. It had been a minute since I'd been waiting for this date. I had filed for the lawsuit on May 11, 2012, and he had to be served again because I didn't have his physical address, I only had his P. O. Box. I drove over to his house and rang his buzzer after I found out that I needed his physical address in order file. He answered the buzzer after I used the call box. He said, "Yes, who is this?" I said, "Is this my former publisher?" He said, "Yes this is," and I just walked away.

I was readier than a motherfucker. I went to the bloggers, and spared no mercy about everything that happened between us. I was letting the world know what this monster was really all about. He was trying to have raw sex with me and I was HIV Positive but he was promoting a book about not having raw sex because of HIV. I wasn't comfortable telling the world my status at first while working with him but he insisted that I do and that is how he was going to brand me.

Shit got real ugly once William McCray from the Obnoxious Radio show (www.Obnoxiousradio.com) got news of what was happening. He was the first person to post a blog and then Lee Bailey from eurweb.com picked it up and it immediately went viral that same night. My former publisher was a well-known name who'd appeared as a guest on the Oprah Winfrey Show twice, and here I was suing his ass. He was using Oprah and Taye Diggs as a selling platform to others.

I had people all up in arms, he had supporters, too. Some people were saying that I was lying and that I was just trying to come up off him. But I didn't give a fuck what anyone thought. The proof was in the pudding and I was airing it all.

To my surprise, I wasn't the only person that publisher had gotten over on, he had taken other people's money, too. This bitch had not only gotten over on me but he had gotten over on about 25 other people. I felt like I really had to do something once I found out. I was so tired of being people's victim so I became the advocate for everyone that couldn't, wouldn't, or was too scared to speak up for themselves. I was going to go first.

So on my court date August 27, 2012 at 1:30 pm I was prepared and sitting in the Fulton County courthouse. I walked in with my black and white pin stripe suit, red, black, and white tie matching my book cover, my Louis Vuitton briefcase with my glasses on. The Judge called my name, and said please approach the podium."

The publisher didn't show up, but I did. Once I made it to the podium, the Judge asked, "Are you representing Samuel Holloway?"

I said, "No your honor, I am Samuel Holloway!" She thought I was a damn lawyer. That's because this bitch was well prepared. I had taken out all my evidence with post it notes attached to each piece of evidence that I had with a number on it.

The Judge who was a Caucasian woman told me to present my case. I went on presenting my case showing her how the publisher did not abide by his contract along with calling out numbers which relative to the evidence I was providing. I had the marshal taking every piece of document back and forth between the Judge and I.

I was very open telling her how we met and how he had took advantage of me by taking nude pictures of me in exchange to lower the contract fee. I was eager to get my story heard but the amount of money he wanted was more than I could afford. I told the Judge how the publisher was trying constantly to have unprotected sex with me knowing I was HIV Positive. I showed her the text messages from my cell phone showing him asking for raw sex, and also pictures that I had taken from my face book messages of him asking for a threesome. All she could say was, "WOW!"

I kept telling her that I was desperate to have my story told, and that in my past I was a prostitute, so he was using sex as a way to hold me back, and not keep-up his end of the contract. I told her that was my past and I no longer live in it, so I was not going to have sex, but I did agree to, only to have the contract met. The contract was never met as a result of me not having sex, so that meant that he breached the contract, and that was the reason I was there today.

After she saw all the evidence presented, she said, "Even if your publisher was here, you would have won by a preponderance of evidence!" "Are you in school young man?" I replied, "Yes your honor." She said, "What is your major?" I stated, "Business

Administration." She said, "I think you need to change that to Law because you would make a great Attorney!" "You presented this case excellent!"

After that, the judge said, "You win by default and a preponderance of evidence!" I was awarded the $15,000 that I had asked for HANDS DOWN! I had wished that the publisher was in attendance because if he was, after we walked out the court room I would have told him, "You can learn a lot from a dummy, dummy!"

******

Before I met this nefarious publisher, I was working with Mina, my first publisher, along with my neighbor, and so called friend Sadaya editing my book. She was a great help catching *some* of the errors. We worked on my book from late April to early August. After we were done I paid her $500 for her assistance. We never discussed a contract or anything, she was just helping me out of the goodness of her heart — at least that's what I thought. She was also an aspiring artist. Her work was great and I had thought of using one of her paintings for my book cover. It's always good to have someone else read your work because we write the same way we speak, proofreaders can catch things that you can't see. She was a great help at first.

I didn't have a cover photo but Sadaya was a great painter and she'd painted a picture that seemed perfect for my book at the time. The black and white picture she produced depicted a figure with no face. It was scary and it captured the attention of my Facebook friends.

After I decided to work directly with the second publisher, I met with and informed Sadaya of my decision and that I would not need her services any longer because this publisher came to the table as an accomplished Gay Author and publisher who had a huge Gay following, a professional editor, and I would also be changing the book cover, and using a portrait of myself. She blew up on the spot. I mean she was livid, and proceeded to let me have it, cursing me out to wits end. She felt that she had put in too much work for me to just blow her off like that. I reiterated that I decided to go with this other publisher since he was well known and most likely to help me follow in his footsteps, becoming a *New York Times* Best Seller.

Her reply was, "So you are just going to drop Mina, and me, and go with a fag that you don't even know?" It pissed me off because she said the word fag. I hate that word and she was being derogatory so I felt some type of way. Short of cursing her ass out, I gave her the check and told her, "Bitch you tried that and your services are no longer needed" and I thanked her. Sadaya and I had never signed a contract, and Mina and I had never discussed what she would be charging me if anything to publish my book.

Sadaya and her cousin Jessica, made messy comments on my Facebook fan page stating that I'm not the author and that she (Sadaya) in fact wrote my book instead of me. Mina said to me. "I told you so." In the beginning that she had a funny feeling about Sadaya, and it wasn't right because she was trying to take over my book. I should have listened to her because she was right from the very beginning.

Sadaya wanted to change the name of several chapters that I had already named, andshe wanted to totally take it over. I told her that this is my story, my book, and my life. If I didn't give her something to correct there's no way in hell she could've even had anything to go off of. I told Sadaya, "Yes, you did correct some of my errors but you did not write my book and you are not the author." I immediately unfriended and blocked both of those bitches. Their friends and family started unfriending me and un-liking my fan page for *Eyes Without a Face* which was fine with me because I was looking for quality, and not the quantity of "LIKES" for support. I never spoke to that bitch, Sadaya since.

She told me that I was going to sink like a shark in the sea without her. I'm showing her daily that I can swim in the sea like the shark and I can't even swim. I sold books without her and continued to do so. Who the hell was she? **Blank Stare**

******

In the midst of my storm, my baby, my child, my cat Tabby died. It was in the afternoon of July 27, 2013. The day before that, Tabby was perfectly fine. We played all day like always. He laid up under me and watched television, but on the 27th I knew something was wrong that afternoon. Tabby just lay in his bed and wouldn't move. He didn't want to eat or drink anything. I was panicking so I called the Veterinarian right away. I knew my little mane contracted respiratory issues that resulted from the house fire back in Minnesota in 2009 and made it difficult for him to breathe.

The Vet told me that they had an appointment available for 6pm that evening. It was almost 3pm and I could tell by the way Tabby looked, he was not going to make it. I picked him up and talked to him, I cried like a baby as I held him. He looked in my eyes the whole time. I know it may sound silly, but I told him how much I loved him, how much he had meant to me. I thanked him for loving me and even thanked him for caring. Tabby was there giving me solace in Dallas, Texas after I was robbed and beaten. He never left my side during that time and now I was not about to leave his either.

Tabby was my only child who'd been in my life since April of 2008. He was only five years old when he passed away. Tabby was the smartest pet that I had known. Price had trained that cat beyond belief. He would come running when I snapped my fingers or called his name. He never went outside, he was just a house cat that loved me. He was friendly to all that entered the house and everyone adored him. He was my "Fat Cat," I call him that because he was a Tabby Cat, known for being chubby. He was white with tan patches. I laid him on my lap until it was time to go to the Vet. He was still holding on to dear life. I felt it within my heart that he was about to leave me. He never made a sound. He just kept looking at me and licking my hand.

I put Tabby in his cat bag and placed it on the back seat of the car. I generally blasted the car radio but on this day I had it turned off. I kept looking back to make sure he was okay for the ride. The Vet was not even five minutes away from my home. As soon as I pulled up and parked the car, I turned around and Tabby was gone, just that fast. I got out the car crying and screaming to the top of my lungs. I felt like my only family here in Atlanta had died and left me all alone. I felt good and bad at the same time. I felt good because I knew my Tabby loved me unconditionally just like I loved him. I knew he waited as long as he could. I felt bad because I would no longer have him in my presence. I felt like that was truly the last part of Price that I held on to as well.

******

I had surgery on my mouth the beginning of August 2013 and was due back for my six-week check-up and removal of sutures on September 12th. In late August, my sutures somehow managed to come out voluntarily after only four weeks. This was unusual so I called and informed my doctor who instructed me to come into his office for a check-up. Upon my arrival, the doctor looked at my mouth and said the infection had totally cleared up and my mouth had healed completely. I remember saying aloud "Glory to GOD," because a brother was starving and hadn't had a decent solid meal in weeks. I had lost almost twenty pounds on that liquid diet mixed with all the excruciating pain I'd endured. The doctor also looked at my mouth to ensure braces could be put on. The dentist gave his okay and signed my paperwork stating that the braces were a go! I was well on my way to smiling completely again.

I scheduled a September 3rd appointment at Orthodontic Care of Georgia where I was already a client. On that day, I became the luckiest man alive and the happiest person in the world, Braces! I was finally getting fitted for my braces and was scheduled to have them placed in my mouth on September 9th. The night before, I was so excited that I could hardly sleep. The surgical wire that was still in my mouth and was taken out by the same Orthodontist during the procedure. I arrived at the Orthodontic Care of Georgia bright and early at 8:15 am. My appointment wasn't until 8:45 am. I was so excited that I just couldn't wait any more at home. The nurse brought me back to the pre prepped surgical room where the Orthodontist awaited my arrival and they immediately began the process. It took less than an hour for them to take the wire out and place the braces on.

My mouth felt so refreshed, but once again, I was in pain. I was told of everything that I could not eat for a couple of weeks which was basically all the good stuff that I like; no chips or candy bars, hell anything in an aluminum bag, gum, steak, caramel, or anything hard. They also said no smoking for the first couple of weeks. I was abiding by everything because this was prudent to me to have my smile back. My smile is my life. I walked out of that dental office feeling like "Sam" once again. I had braces and my teeth were about to be as they were almost three years ago to that date.

CHAPTER 14

GOD FAVORED ME

After my fourth surgery on August 10, 2013 I realized I was still hurting in some sort of way. I couldn't pin point my feelings or frustrations, but I knew this pain was deeply rooted within my soul. I found myself on an emotional roller coaster, fighting with my own mind. I was trying to convince myself that I was fine and that I had completely healed, but that was a lie. If you're still living, your life on earth isn't complete. With negative thoughts racing through your mind with demonic influences, they weigh you down into a state of depression. People can have the same effect on you, that's bondage a form of spiritual warfare. That spiritual warfare in my case was the negativity from my family

In March of 2001, at 22, I was raped, and that November I was diagnosed with Depression, however I believe I was depressed long before I was raped. You see, after being beaten by my mother because her boyfriend molested me at ten years old and not knowing what that fully meant; I took the title but not the meaning of what "Depression" really is. I couldn't see this disease, nor did I feel its effects every day, they only hit me during Holidays and special events. After the break up with my husband Price in April of 2010, I felt and knew what depression really was as it now consumed my whole being. I didn't think I would return from the state of mind I was in; but I did, it just took time. But I never fully recovered from it.

Not even a full seven months later, I was dealing with another form of Depression. I was depressed for two reasons; the way I looked and what my husband had, had done to me. I was set up, robbed and beaten by the men who were sleeping with him. They beat the right side of my body till it went numb, my left eye was swollen shut and just trying to open it caused a stabbing pain that made me see stars. I felt excruciating pain coursing through every fiber my body. My mouth and jaw were exposed and the pain throbbed with each beat of my heart. It felt like nothing I'd ever experienced before. Once again, Depression took over and when I moved to Atlanta in December of 2010 I began taking depression medication for the first time. A simple pill each night called Celextra and the pill made me feel so happy. It made all the pains of depression go away so I took that pill faithfully until I started feeling better.

The side effects started kicking in and not knowing how depression works, I was feeling sad, depressed more than ever, suicidal, lonely, and unloved along with a lot of other feelings. On April 29, 2014 I tried the unspeakable to end my life. I was crying off and on all day. I couldn't pin point it, but I knew something wasn't right. I felt that would be the only way to make those feelings go away. I had suppressed so much that I was literally going crazy. Everything that I thought I'd forgotten was coming back full fledged. It wasn't just in dreams anymore it was consuming me.

I could be watching something or someone could say something and there came flying a memory. I found myself talking to myself sometimes. I was talking to myself so much that I had to look in the mirror and say, "Bitch Shut Up!" As the day progressed, my feelings evolved more. I started to shut down mentally feeling like I didn't want to be here anymore. By 9pm I began my escape route from this life, which I felt was so horrible. I cleaned my home from top to bottom because I didn't want anyone to find me with my home being unpresentable. That's what happens when you have OCD.

By 11pm, I started praying hard and asking GOD to forgive me in advance. I got my Bible out and started to read certain verses. I cried more and prayed harder. I tried calling people but no one that I wanted to talk to would answered. I wasn't looking for someone to save me, I really just wanted to say goodbye without saying goodbye.

I grabbed a piece of cardboard from the box that my books were delivered in and began to write. It was perfect in size for what I needed to get off my chest. I apologized to family; specially my nieces and nephew. I felt that I had given up on them more than myself. I felt bad but I still needed to do this. I couldn't take the pain that I was feeling anymore. I realized I'd lost my battle to continue to live and I cried out to my GOD! I cried so hard and long and by 12:29am I'd prayed all that I could pray. I didn't know how long I had been crying until I looked at the clock. I had cried and prayed for almost an hour and a half and it was now time to go.

I got my pill bottles from the bathroom drawer. I laid them all on the bed. I had a total of six different kinds of pills. Some were old and some were brand new and still sealed while others had already been opened. I had two different types of HIV pills. I had an old bottle of Atripala, which I was no longer taking and two bottles of Stribold, the bottle I was on and a new prescription. I had my new bottle of sleeping pills, Ambien, as well as a new bottle of Lexapro for my depression, along with Oxycodone, which were leftover from my last surgery.

I poured all the pills out of their bottles and onto the bed. I had a little over 160 pills, which I placed in groups of 20 and had a bottle of water sitting on the nightstand. After looking at the pills, I broke down crying. The realization of what I was about to do was setting in. I cried out louder for my GOD to stop me if I wasn't supposed to commit this terrible act upon myself. I knew HE was listening but HE didn't give me any type of sign not to go ahead with this. I then turned off all the lights in my house and sat on the side of my bed with my Bible in hand.

I held the closed Bible tightly. It was the bible that my sister had given to me for a birthday gift the prior year, which had my name engraved in it. I felt so bad but I knew at this point I was making the right decision. By this time, it was now a little after 2am and I was ready to go. I took the first set, which were 20 Ambien pills. After that, I took the next set of 20 Oxycodone pills. I immediately felt light headed and sleepy. I continued to sit on the floor Indian style with my Bible still in my hands.

I cried more and prayed too as I realized what I had just done. I couldn't stop now because I had already taken 40 pills. I figured if I stopped, it could have horrible side effects from the pills and I didn't want to live now so why would I want to live through that? I immediately took the next set of 20 pills which were my old HIV medicine, Atripala. After taking those, I laid across the bed with my Bible still clutched into my arms. I was crying saying I was sorry out loud because I knew that I was going to die from what I was doing.

I started to take my next set of 20 pills and chocked on them. I chocked so hard that they only went halfway down my throat and came right back up. I kept them in my hand as I cried and ran into the kitchen to get another bottle of water in a daze. After returning to the bedroom, I got on my knees on the side of the bed. I gathered the remaining pills, and took them in groups of 20. As soon as I finished my last batch, I prayed, stopped crying, and lay in bed clutching the Bible in my arms tightly until I passed out.

******

It was around nine in the morning and I kept hearing this ringing noise. I was so incoherent that I couldn't even answer the phone. I started vomiting right away but it wasn't vomit, it was blood! I was throwing up blood everywhere. I tried running to the bathroom and passed out right at the toilet. I don't remember getting up to get my phone, or even remember if I had it with me the whole time in my hand. TaQuan was calling but I didn't know who he was when I answered.

He kept asking me was I okay? Apparently one of my friends was calling him asking had he heard from me, because we had an exam at school and I wasn't there. My friend knew it wasn't like me to miss school, let alone an exam. I was crying and vomiting at the same time trying to reply. Finally I was able to get out that I had taken a lot of pills and I tried to commit suicide. He asked for my address and I gave it to him ultimately. Within seconds the police were calling me. The lady on the phone was trying to keep me on the phone until help arrived. Within minutes the fire department and police were at my front door and entering my home. My front door must have been unlocked through the entire night.

They brought me into my room where they sat me down on the bed, got me dressed and placed me on the stretcher. I was rushed to the hospital where everything went blank. I could only remember flash backs of people surrounding me in the ambulance and hospital room. I saw all types of machines that I was hooked to. I felt no pain. I was truly at ease. I was in and out of consciousness and I couldn't stop crying because I had failed at trying to kill myself. All I could think was why had GOD forsaken me and I was pissed!

******

After coming too but still being under the influence of the medication I had taken, the doctor started asking me all types of questions and telling me what I had done to myself internally. She told me that I would eventually heal but I had done some damage. First off, she said my blood pressure was 70/50 and that I could have had a stroke. She said I was near death and everything else was just question after question. I didn't really care because I wasn't dead. My stomach was in severe pain. After I answered them, I had to see a Psychiatrist with a new set of questions; like was I depressed or anything of that nature. I explained to her that I had been depressed now for years off and on. I have my good days and I have my bad days and this for sure was one of my bad days I told her. After her interview, she decided that I should go to an institution for observations and treatment over the next 72 hours. I agreed with her but I had no idea of what was about to come.

After that, they placed me in a cold empty room without a piece of carpet, a bed, TV, telephone, string, dust, not even a window, just a camera in the corner of the celling. Now there was a mattress like a cot without the metal frame on the floor with a sheet for me to lie on. The nurse told me I had to eat something so the food could absorb the pills. She gave me a ham sandwich with an apple and one of them hospital juices, which was an apple juice. I tried and ate a little but before long I passed out again. I was eating like I was drunk.

I was awakened by an older heavyset Caucasian man and young heavyset Caucasian woman. They were taking me to the institution. I was strapped down on another stretcher even though I continued to tell them that the restraints were unnecessary because I wasn't crazy and that these measures were a bit much. The lady stated, "Unfortunately, due to the situation, the restraints are needed." I didn't say anything; I just lay back with tears falling from my eyes.

I started thinking to myself, "What the hell had I done?" I was shaking because I was cold in spite of it being hot outside. They loaded me into an old 80's style ambulance as the lady started talking to me and the man began driving. She was taking my vitals and marking them down on a clipboard. She told me that everything was going to be okay and she too had done what I tried to do years ago. She said she also had been to the place where I was going. I just laid back and listened to her and soon fell asleep until the man said, "We're here!"

When I arrived at the institution, they unloaded and wheeled me inside. I sat in a waiting area until I was checked me in. I was freezing. I only had on basketball shorts, tee shirt, and socks, No Shoes. It was around 1 am when I arrived the next day on April 30th. A tall black man dressed in regular street clothes came out of an office. He took me to another smaller room and began to ask me questions like, what's my full name, address, date of birth, social security number and other things. Lastly before he walked out of the room, he took a head shot of me. After he was done asking me questions, he told me to follow him back to the waiting room area. While sitting there, I happened to look up and I noticed all the security cameras on the ceiling. I felt like I was in the Juvenile Detention Center like when my mom had me arrested for being gay.

That's when it fully hit me: "I was in a crazy house." There were other people waiting to go into the facility also. Now some of them really looked like they were crazy, but I knew I was not. I was looking around like, "What The Fuck?!" I had to go through intake to get to where I needed to be within the facility. The Intake Nurse came out of the double doors in the waiting area and called my name.

She told me to follow her. She was a black, heavy set, Jamaican lady from her accent, dressed in a green nurse uniform with a stethoscope around her neck. We walked down this long quite hall. It was just straight with tiled flooring and plastic looking walls and was real dim. I didn't know if it was just me or was I just high as hell from all those damn pills I had taken, but the hallway had this creepy feeling to it.

Once we got into her office, she started asking me all types of questions. She was asking questions like, "Had I ever tried to commit suicide before?" Not knowing what this place was, my dumb ass replied, "Yes!" I wasn't able to get into my room until around 4am the next morning, so the intake nurse told me to seat in the hallway until someone came to get me. She told me that the people working there were called Mental Health Assistants (MHA). After intake, I was told that I would be taken to the hall called "The E Hall" until my bed was ready, but they had to give me a bed for now. The E hall meant the "Psychotic Hall," I would soon find out!

I had to sit in this area where there was a nurse desk in front of me. There were two black women working behind the counter.

They both had on blue nurse's uniforms. They paid me no attention while I sat there. While I was sitting there, I saw a hall behind me and in another in front of me. I saw different women walking back and forth. They were Black, Latino, and Caucasian women. Some had on hospital gowns, others were in saggy clothes. Some had on shoes with no shoestrings; others didn't have any shoes on at all, just socks. No one dressed had on any belts. They were either sagging, or holding their pants up to keep them from falling off of them.

Some women were talking to themselves, some were crying and some just looked off into space. I knew two things for sure; one, they all were staring at me, and two, they all seemed crazy as ever. I was scared as fuck. However, I had to man up because I didn't want any dumb shit to happen to me. I tried my best to be alert as possible. Unfortunately I had taken too many damn pills and I seemed drunk. One of the ladies asked the nurses behind the desk what time was breakfast? I swear they acted like no one had said anything and kept right on doing what they were doing.

I was so tired and sleepy, hungry, and thirsty. I asked the nurses if I could have something to eat or drink. They both looked at each other then looked at me. Then one of the nurses said, "We don't serve breakfast until 8:45 am with a smart ass tone." I said, "Okay, thank you," very politely as I could try to talk. "Well may I have something to drink please?" One of the nurses said yes, there's water behind you or you can have a juice. I asked for the juice and she handed me a little juice cup from a refrigerator behind them. She really only gave me one.

Soon as I finished the extra small apple juice, a tall dark skin man walked from out the double doors in front of me which was the "E Hall." I may have been under the influence, but he was fine as hell to be dark skin. **I know I was in a mental institution** He called my name but I was the only person sitting there, but he still called my name anyway. **Blank Stare** I got up, and he started walking back towards the hall he had just left from. He turned around and started walking, so I assumed that meant to follow him, so I did. We had to be buzzed in to get back in through the double doors.

Once through the double doors, I was in a whole different world. What I had just witnessed with the women talking, crying and looking off into space was nothing compared to what I was now seeing. This had to be the men's hall because I didn't see any women. There were some ugly men, some fine men, and some very fine men. There were old men and young men. There was nothing on that hall but men period from the patients to the workers.

I was scared as hell because these men were staring at me, yelling, throwing things, talking and touching themselves, too. I immediately asked the man that was walking me to my room, "Am I in the right place?" He looked at me said, "You will be okay, I will look out for you and my name is Abdul." I told Abdul, "I'm scared as fuck bro!" I was at attention like a motherfucker. The drugs hadn't worn off, but I was at fully alert, in fear of my life. I thought, "One of these crazy motherfuckers may try and run up on me and I was going to let they ass have it!"

As Abdul and I approached room 105, he told me that this was going to be my room until they have a bed ready on the "B Hall!" I said okay until I walked in the room. As soon as I walked in the room, there was an older heavyset black man lying on the bed by the door, naked with the sheet in between his legs. I yelled out, "Oh Hell Naw!" Abdul called the guy by his name and told him to put some clothes on but the guy didn't move nor did he say anything.

Fuck that! I told Abdul right then and there, "I am not supposed to be over here! I am not crazy bro!" Abdul said unfortunately that there were no beds available yet and I would have to wait until one becomes available to move.

He pointed me in the direction of my bed and said he would be checking on me every hour. I wanted him to check every fucking minute, I was scared as shit. There was no light in the room; the light came from the hallway. There was a shared toilet just like prison with a curtain to hide it. The room reeked of urine. To make matters worse, the guy sharing the room with me was staring at me when I lay down on the bed. He was facing directly towards me and was naked. I thought I was going to have a damn heart attack because my heart was beating so fast.

I laid down that night and passed out. I was scared but the drugs over powered me. I awoke to a man asking me my name and date of birth. He looked like he was either from India or Saudi Arabia. He told me to follow him. We went into this little room still on the same hall and he introduced himself as Dr. Ian. He asked me what I did to be in here. I thought, I know they told you. I know your ass read my chart! He was trying to play games with me. So I just said, "I was extremely sleepy from studying for school and I took a lot of sleeping pills."

As soon as I said that, he asked, "Was that it?" I said, "Yes." He then told me to go back to my room. I asked right away, "When am I going to be released?" This motherfucker said, "I'm not sure yet?" What the fuck, I thought to myself. I was pissed off. I went back to my room and wrapped myself under the sheet. I had totally blocked out the madness going on around me. These people didn't even exist. I just wanted to hurry and get the fuck out of here like

ASAP! I knew that I had just tried to commit suicide but I didn't want to think about it nor say it.

Later that day before Abdul left to go home, he told me I would be transferring to the B Hall later because a bed had become available. I was happy as hell although I was in a crazy place. Abdul really looked out for me. Everyone had to eat in the little room that was on the hall for breakfast, lunch and dinner. But when they called me to come for breakfast after I left from seeing the doctor, I didn't want to go into the room with a lot of crazy men. I wasn't stupid and they were not about to do whatever they were thinking of doing to me. Even if they weren't thinking about me, I was thinking about me for them. I wasn't going. I told Abdul I would starve until I was moved. He wasn't having that and allowed me to eat in the room and brought me some food.

Later that evening I was moved onto the B Hall. I had to stay on the E Hall for lunch and dinner. The next shift MHA was Brandon. Abdul brought him to the room and introduced us to each other. Abdul told me that Brandon would watch out for me until I was moved. I was so grateful for Abdul, he was a Godsend. I actually believe the guy that I shared the room with was Heaven sent to in his own way. He never spoke and he stared at me the entire time I was in that room. I feel like he was watching over me because he knew I was scared out of my mind.

Brandon and I walked through the E Hall, to the C Hall, I passed so many differently personalities. I felt bad because I had actually called people crazy and had never really seen a crazy person in real life until now. We always judge what we don't know, and now I knew for sure what crazy really was. Insane is another word I'd like to say instead and I saw insane while I was there through different people.

We had finally arrived in the B Hall. That was a long walk, and we had to pass a lot of locked doors to get there. The only way through every other door was if you had a key or by being buzzed in. The security was tight so no one could escape. When Brandon and I entered the next hall, I saw a different side of people. I saw people that were just like me. They were on the phones on the wall having conversations; they were talking to each other and just acting normal. Some of them looked mad, sad and some were crying. I knew their actions were solely based on the fact that they didn't want to be there.

It was mandatory that patients stay here if they're brought here. Only a doctor could release you, but only after you spent a maximum of 72 hours. If the 72 hours fell on a weekend, that didn't count. You also had to sign a release form against your doctor's orders to be released. However, the release form only went into effect after the 72 hours had expired. The release form gave the facility permission to release you upon your wishes but only after the 72 hours had passed and 48 hours after that for the release form to expire. They wanted to ensure they were covered if you would try to commit suicide being that you were just released. Those tricky bastards made you stay in there for a total of five days before a doctor would actually release you.

Right as Brandon was taking me into the group meeting room where everyone was, I felt a spirit of relief. I was terrified on the E Hall and to be around normal people on this end felt so much better. These people were just like me; a person with psychological problems. When you try and take your own life, you do have a serious mental issue. That was so hard for me to admit out loud, but I knew it deep within. There had to be like about 25 people sitting around in chairs and little two seat chairs that looked like small futons. The room had games like checkers, cards, dominos, newspapers, magazines, puzzle and drawing paper along with makers and crayons. The setting was peaceful.

There were black, white, Asian, men, and women in the circle. There were young people as young as 18 and older people as old at 72. After being there a couple of days, I learned everyone's name, age and reason why they were there. I sat in the group waiting for it to start. There were two MHA's in the circle. They had a clipboard and pen in their hands. They also wore blue and green nurse's uniforms. As the group began, everyone became silent and you could hear a pin drop.

One of the MHA's began speaking to everyone in the room. She said, "Alright everyone, this is the cool down for the evening. I want everyone to state your goals from this morning, were they accomplished and how do you rate yourself." She then asked if anyone wanted to start off. No one volunteered, so she told the person next to her to start. Ms. Susan was an elderly Caucasian woman, the oldest person in the room. That's exactly what she said after she said her name. She stated that her goal was to talk to her husband and sister, and tell them about her ordeal, and why she had tried to commit suicide.

Ms. Susan had stated that as a baby, her mother sodomized her. Her mother broke both of her hands, fingers and legs before she was even two years old. She also said that her mother would put things inside her vagina. The abuse carried on until Ms. Susan was 16 years old. She ended up running away because the abuse became too intense for her. She has a sister whom the mother didn't abuse and their relationship was not so well due to that fact. The sister believed that the abuse was normal.

After going through many years with no counseling or anyone to talk, Ms. Susan said she broke. She turned to alcohol and prescription drugs to numb her pain. She stood up when she spoke. She made sure her voice was heard and her story was told. She had tears flowing, but she didn't cry out loud. She was a strong woman in my eyes. I related to her and her story almost instantly. It brought tears to my eyes. Ms. Susan said that she had gotten very sad over the last couple months and the doctors had told her that she had depression. She also stated that she had just had breast surgery to remove one of her breasts and she was a cancer survivor. She said she had met her goals after speaking with her husband and sister and had set up a family visit for that coming Tuesday. She rated herself a 10 for the evening.

I was thinking, "Damn, now that was a story. Here I am complaining and I hadn't been through half the shit that she had!" The next person was a young girl was named Tina. She looked every bit of 18 to 20 years old. She was a beautiful girl. She was black and mixed with something. She had a short cut and spoke so well. He eyes said she was going through hell. Tina also stood up and spoke. She was so articulate.

Tina stated that she had not met her goal today. Her goal was to find somewhere to stay after leaving the clinic. She was new to Atlanta from New York and didn't have family here in town. She stated that she was trying to get moved over to "The Lodge" after being discharged from Anchor. Anchor was the name of the place that we were in. It was a mental abuse facility. The Lodge was a place after treatment at Anchor that was a free to come and go as you please facility.

Tina began to tell her story. She said that she was only 18 years old. She said that she had been having sex since she was around

5 or 6 years old but didn't know exactly when it began, but it was going on while she was 6 years old for sure. Tina said her mother was a druggy and used to sell her for crack to drug dealers. She said that they would have sex with her while her mother sat right there and did her drugs. She didn't know who her father was and had never met him.

As Tina had gotten older, around 8 years old her mother had another little girl. Tina said she had been having sex quite often by that time and was used to it. Tina said once she turned 16 years old, her sister was turning 8 years old. She said that's why her mother tried to sell her baby sister for drugs and she jumped on her mother and called child protective services. She reported her mother and CPS took her and her sister immediately. Tina said she and her sister and were spilt up, and she hadn't seen her since.

When Tina turned 18, she said she was released from CPS. She stated that she was never adopted and spent two years in a group home. After her release, she began having sex to take care of her. She said she was used to it because she had already done it for many years. I began to understand and relate to her story. I kind of did the same thing too. She then went on to say that the pain and depression kicked in and became too much to bear. To cope with it, she began to cut herself. Tina said she started with razor blades, and then went to broken glass, and finally just anything she could use to cut herself with.

By that time, tears were coming out of my eyes. I felt so bad because she was so young. I had always said, "We all have a story within us!" I was so right. I couldn't believe these stories as the circle continued; it was now my turn. I had been thinking of something to say all the while others were speaking and while listening to them. I began by saying hello to everyone. I introduced myself as Samuel.

Not everyone stood up, but I felt I needed too. Here I was living this perfect life, painting this beautiful picture to others when inside I was a wreck. I was torn up and pretending to be happy. I was sad and happy some days and mad and glad others. Some days were good days and some days were bad days. I then went on to say the following while I stood up.

"I can't believe that I am here at Anchor; a place where people have to go that are a danger to themselves, or society; a place where people go for drug, alcohol abuse treatment, or attempted suicide. A place where people go that is really for crazy people. The life that I'm living and the things I'm doing to help others, I can't believe that I am the one who needs help right now. My life just turned upside down within a matter of hours. I tried to commit suicide because of the pain that I was feeling from deep within. I can so relate too many of your stories. I apologize that any of us had to go through something so terrible. Being here right now, listening to everyone, I do feel that I am in the right place at the right time. I needed help and I didn't know how to ask. Just like many of you here, I turned to things to ease or numb my pain. I chose alcohol, and marijuana. I then used the prescription medication that was supposed to help my pain I used to try and kill myself. While I walked through each hall trying to get here to be with you all, I realized something so valuable. Life is valuable. We are all here telling our stories, our pains. However, those people on the C and E Halls, can't or won't tell their story. Not because they don't want too, but because it's too late for them too. Some of them can't speak, and some just have major issues and it has become too late to help them. But us, we were saved by the Grace of GOD. HE allowed us to get this far just so we can help save someone else. I'm happy to be on this side with you all today. I could actually be on one of those halls instead!"

As the tears began to roll down my face, I began to feel a weight lifted off my shoulders. I began to feel free all because I was talking about my story, and by hearing others. I knew that we could all help each other. That's why we were all there at that same place and time. We didn't judge each other nor talk down about the next person's actions to get them put into Anchor.

While the days rolled by, I was getting more anxious to leave. The weekend had passed and it was now Monday. I was finally able to make phone calls. I actually didn't want to be there but I knew I needed professional help. Sometimes it was just too much being there in that place. Every day at 5am, the nurses would wake us up to get our vitals. They would come to each room and say, "Vitals Get Up!" That used to piss me off. I hate being woken up out of my sleep. To make matters worse, the MHA's that worked over nights, checked in on us every hour. They shined a flashlight in our faces to make sure we were alive I guess.

I didn't remember any phone numbers except my cousin Felicia's, my straight homeboy Onesimus', and Timothy's. The MHA had told me that I could make phone calls at certain times but all long distance calls could only be made from 7 pm to 9 pm. I was irritated as hell. I hadn't talked to any of my friends or family since that Thursday when I tried to kill myself. I knew people were worried about me.

My cell phone was brought with me when I went into the hospital. One of the paramedics had placed it on my stretcher bed but when I got checked in at Anchor, they locked my phone up, and said I couldn't have access to it. My doctor had given the MHA an order to allow me to go through my phone to get phone numbers. I would have to have a family meeting with either family, or friends in order to be released. I had to have some goals as to how I was going to handle my depression going forward, versus trying to kill myself. They called our goals, "Coping skills."

I knew what got me to that place to where I thought death would be better. I was going through it with a lot of things. I was dealing with Depression, PTSD, my dreams, a marriage that I wanted a divorce from badly, my mother, my family, some of my friends, HIV and just life in general. Through all of this, I know now that making an appointment with a counselor or therapist, calling a family member, or friend, could have helped, and will help me going forward. I was so selfish to try and take my life when I didn't give it to myself. What the fuck was I thinking, I thought to myself.

After going through my phone, I got the numbers out that I needed. I ended up speaking to Felicia, my sister, Timothy, Onesimus, TaQuan and Kevin all while I was there. Of course everyone said just about the same thing. "You know you could have called me if you felt you needed to talk!" Everyone said the same thing, but no one snapped on me just at that moment when they had first heard from me. The snapping came days later or a little after asking was I okay. It felt so good to hear familiar voices.

******

The first person I called was Kevin. Part of the reason that I was there was because of him too. Our phone call seemed so awkward to me. Although I needed his help, I was kind of mad that I even had to talk to him. During our brief conversation, Kevin told me that he had reached out to one of my cousins on Facebook and told them what happened. He said he felt that he needed to tell someone in my family. I asked Kevin who did he tell, and he said that he told this girl that had commented on one of our pictures that he and I had taken together.

Kevin told me said that she posted "Nice picture cousin," so he assumed we were related and told her. I told him that was cool. He then said my mom had called him because the person that he told contacted her. He said that my mom was talking crazy and saying things like, "Somebody set my baby up, someone did something to him because he is not the same and that she was on her way to Atlanta!" During the midst of their phone call, Kevin said my sister called him. He hung up from my mother and my sister told him that she would let the family know and for him to keep her updated about me.

Kevin then stated that Timothy and TaQuan had reached out to him also. He said that he went over my house to check on it because I had given him the keys to my place and car earlier in the year. He said everything was okay and that he had found and taken the suicide letter that I had written with him. I thanked him and told him that he could keep my car while I was there. Kevin had planned on coming to visit me during Family Day on Tuesday May 6th. By that time I had been there for five days now.

******

In February, Kevin told all of his gay friends that his nephew was moving down from Virginia in March to live with Quinton and him. Kevin went on to say that he didn't want any of his friends to talk to his nephew. He felt his nephew was straight, too young, and it would ruin his friendship with us.

I thought differently. Not that I wanted him at all, I just felt that his nephew was a grown man; he was 21 years old with a child. He was able to make his own decisions. He was attractive, tall around 5'10", 150 pounds and of course; a redbone. His nephew had come onto me repeatedly and I finally gave in. I found out from Kevin that his nephew wanted to have sex with me but before Kevin could tell me this, his nephew told me first.

Kevin's nephew hit me up on Facebook the night we went out to the club. Well it was actually at 5:59 am the next morning. He and Kevin stayed up talking and that's when he told his uncle that if he was gay, he would be with Sam and would fuck Sam too. Kevin, Quinton, George, Kevin's nephew and I, had all gone out the club "Bull Dogs" which is the hottest gay club here in Atlanta. That entire night Kevin's nephew was under me like we went together. All my friends knew that anytime someone tries to talk to me and if I'm not interested, I usually grab the closest friend and say, "This is my boyfriend!"

I had been doing that for the entire two years that we all had known each other. That's what happened when some guy grabbed and was trying to talk to me. I didn't grab anyone, but Kevin's nephew was standing behind me. The guy that was trying to talk to me asked was that my man, because dude was mean mugging him. I told him yes, and he walked away. That's when I felt that Kevin's nephew had liked me.

A few weeks had gone by and Kevin started asking me to take his nephew to job interviews, the store, picking him from work once he got a job and a lot more. I was cool with it because I was help-ing my friend because he and his boyfriend's work schedule didn't permit them to take his nephew places sometimes. My attraction to him wasn't physical. My attraction came from being around him all the time and discovering his personality and we became friends and we formed a natural bond outside of Kevin.

When Kevin's nephew came on to me the first time, out of respect for my friend Kevin, I didn't take the bait. After some days had passed I went over to Kevin's house to have brunch on Sunday like we always do, Kevin was at work but the rest of us were there. Quinton, and one of his friends, George, Kevin's nephew and I were watching the Real Housewives of Atlanta on TV. After a while, Kevin's nephew went upstairs to his room. He started texting me, and asking me to come up stairs. I kept saying I was watching the TV. After like five or so texts, I ended up going up stairs into his room falling into a trap. I walked in the room and he had his shorts down with his dick out lying across his bed.

Before I knew it, I ended up giving him fellatio for a couple of minutes. I did it until he was fully erect. I stopped myself because I had not told him my HIV status and because I was in Kevin's house giving his nephew head. Kevin knew my status but his nephew didn't. After I stopped, I told him that I was HIV positive. Even after I told Kevin's nephew I was HIV positive, he still didn't care, he wanted to continue. He wanted to stay overnight at my house to have sex because he was living with Kevin. I declined because I felt that it was inappropriate since we had just met not even two full months ago, and that had gone way further than I'd expected it to go. His nephew started sending me pictures of his dick and body. I felt that part of the reason that I had gave in, was because Kevin basically forced us to be together.

The next day I had gone to Mary Mac's Tea Room in Atlanta to have lunch. I met Kevin, Quinton, George and Kevin's nephew. Lunch was very different to say the least. Our crew was normally talkative, laughing, looking at men and shading each other, but today was quite different. We were almost silent through the entire lunch before we departed. However, under the table the nephew and I rubbed legs a couple of times and kept looking into each other's eyes.

Kevin called me the next day and we exchanged words over the phone because of it. I barely had gotten a chance to say anything because Kevin took over the conversation. He threw out comments like; I was desperate, and how could I do such a thing? I felt really bad, but even after I told him that his nephew came on to me first, it really didn't matter to him. Kevin felt his nephew was still a child and confused about his sexuality. I felt that Kevin's nephew was grown and making his own decisions, but I also understand where Kevin was coming from because that was his nephew.

******

After that I called Onesimus. I could only call those who were local because of the rules at the facility. Onesimus said that he had been calling and calling my friends to see where I was because I had missed an exam. I told him what happened. He was like, "OMG, bro you could have called me, I would have talked to you!" Onesimus said, "Bro I love you mane and you know you got people in your corner." I ended the call with Onesimus because the MHA said that a Teresa was on the phone for me. That was my sister!

I took the call from my sister on the same phone after the MHA transferred the call over. She was very disappointed. Kevin had contacted my cousin on Facebook because he didn't know who to contact. He was my emergency contact for the hospital. He found out through them and from TaQaun. My sister said that Kevin told my cousin what happened, who in turn told the rest of the family. At that point, I didn't even care, I was dealing with a lot and I let that roll right off. My sister was very concerned and asked did she need to come to ATL. Just like my sister being a mother because

I didn't have one. I mean I had one, she just was not active like a mother should be; but I still loved my mother with all my heart. I loved my sister so much, but I declined the offer. This was something that I would have to deal with. My sister also said that her and my brother had planned to come. They were the main two trying to come check on they brother, we are all we have, and she and I talked for the maximum of 30 minutes that was allowed.

My sister told me that she contacted the family members that Kevin contacted. My brother had told her who all knew. My sister made sure she told everyone little as possible because she knew that I wouldn't want some of my family in my business. Some of them were just waiting on my downfall and this was the perfect time for them to get what they wanted. I thanked her. Although at that point I didn't really care about too much, I still cared a little being that I didn't die. After we hung up, I asked one of the MHA's that was real cool, if I could a couple more long distance calls. I explained to her that I had been in Anchor since Friday at 4am and it was Monday and I was just getting in contact with my friends and family. She allowed me to have access to the phone to continue to make my calls.

My sister then told me to call Felicia or Nina because they both were worried. I called Felicia and she sounded so happy to hear from me. Felicia said, "Lil Holly, (that's what she called me), it feels good to know your alive! Do you know you had us worried sick because we hadn't heard from you?" It made me feel bad because I knew I was being selfish and my family was going to have the burden of knowing that I took my own life. I apologized and told her I would never do that again. She made me promise to call her more now than ever before so she would know that I was in the right state of mind. I promised and we said our good byes.

The next person on the list was TaQaun. I called him and the first thing he asked was, "Are you okay Sam?" I told him I was now. TaQuan said that I had scared the shit out of him when he spoke to me. I didn't even remember that we had spoken. I remembered hearing his voice at one point but I had forgotten that he was the one that called the police until he told me. He said he was ready to take a flight after I told him that I just tried to commit suicide. It brought tears to my eyes because it put me back in reality of what exactly I tried to do.

It was at that moment that TaQuan snapped on me. TaQuan told me he didn't care what life had thrown at me. I had better dodge shit the next time being that I had already dodged so much other stuff. TaQuan said, "You are one of the strongest people that I know. You've been through so much and you decided to take the higher road." I explained to him everything that took place and why I was there at Anchor. TaQuan said, "Bitch, I'm going to need you to get it together because you can overcome anything like you always have." He then ended the call by saying, "I love you and I will always be by your side!"

I hung up with tears in my eyes and called Timothy and by this time, I was crying. This was the first time that I had cried since being admitted to Anchor. Everything was coming back to me when I was in the hospital but I continued my call to Timothy. He was my best friend and I really needed him at that point. As soon as he picked up, he said, "Sam!" I was like, "Damn bitch, yes it's me!" He made me smile right away and my tears instantly dried up. Timothy said, "Girl I love you so much! Don't you ever pull any shit like this again or I'm going to kill you my damn self!" We laughed so hard, that was my very first time laughing while in Anchor. I went through the motions with Timothy on the phone.

The MHA said I had only 10 minutes left before we had another group session so I had to wrap our call up. I was so happy that I had spoken to everyone. It made me feel a lot better, but at the same time I felt ashamed that everyone knew what I had done, but I knew it really didn't matter because they all loved me.

******

It was now visitation day. This day couldn't have come soon enough. I was so ready to go home and this day was key to my release. Kevin came and we had an entire hour to just talk. It felt good seeing him because he was my friend. I had known him a little over two years at that point. We sat at a table in the cafeteria with the rest of the people that were at Anchor along with their family and friends. Kevin told me the hospital story, which fucked me up. Kevin said that he, Quinton, George and his nephew rushed to the hospital after TaQuan called and told him what happened. He said that everyone had taken off work and met up at the hospital. Kevin said they went to the front desk where they were directed to the emergency room. Kevin was my emergency contact person so the doctor came out and spoke with him. Kevin said that the doctor had told him that it didn't look good and they were working on me.

He said that's when he got nervous and started reaching out to my family. In fact, I had died on the table and the doctors revived me. That brought back the memories that I had in the hospital when TaQuan first brought up the conversation. I remembered waking up to tubes being placed down my throat, throwing up in the hospital and seeing lots of blood. I promise I saw the "White Light." That "White Light" is real when people say that they died and came back. I truly believe that because that's exactly what I had experienced. I had a sore on my nose from blood coming out my nose, a broken toe because I passed out trying to walk while I was in the house and stitches on my elbow after I collapsed.

Kevin told me that they were going to make sure I was okay once I was released and we would put this all behind us. However, Kevin said that George felt an intervention was necessary. In my mind, I was thinking, "What the fuck I need an intervention for? Because I almost fucked your nephew?! No, you bitches need an intervention because…"

Instantly, I snapped out of it because the new medication I was on was about to put me in a different state of mind. My doctor had prescribed me Lexapro for my depression and right at that moment I was starting to feel depressed. I quickly changed the subject and we began talking about the stay at Anchor. After about fifteen more minutes, visitation was over and Kevin and I hugged and he left.

******

The last few days were good and bad. I was actually enjoying it because I had met so many people from different walks of life and a lot of strong people were there. Yes, some of them may have tried to commit suicide, or were drug or alcohol abusers, but they were seeking help. We all had problems. We all exchanged each other's information. We talked and encouraged one another and lifted each other up throughout the days we were there. We played spades, did puzzles, colored things, and even played jeopardy with games about how to cope with our issues.

The reasons I didn't want to be there were many. It was always cold for one. I hated the cold weather so of course I didn't want to be in a facility where it was cold 24/7. I didn't like the fact that I had to take the depression medication. It did make me feel better mentally, but physically it had me super tired throughout the day.

I didn't like not being able to call my friends and family when I wanted to. I hated seeing the mentally unstable people, it made me sad and I often wondered what their lives were like before Anchor.

I had started smoking cigarettes again while in there. We had six smoke breaks throughout the day. The people in there were getting cigarettes brought to them by their family's I assumed, but I bummed a cigarette every chance I could. We were so cool that most of the times they just offered them to me. I hated that I could only brush my teeth two times a day. We could only have our toiletries first thing in the morning and right before we went to bed. We only ate three times a day and the food was horrible but I needed to brush my teeth because of my braces after every meal and couldn't. I couldn't shave because we couldn't have sharp items and I became a werewolf after my third day there.

I hated going to the C Hall, where we would have group sessions with the people over there. They combined B and C Halls twice a day to talk about our issues and what we would do differently so we wouldn't end up back in Anchor. They really had crazy people over there. There were three women in particular that really scared me.

The three women, who were all black, would say the same things over and over and over again like clockwork. It was bothering me so much. It kept replaying in my head for a moment. It made me think of my mother. My mother would say some things over and over again and I felt that she was going to be just like them if she didn't seek help soon. The only good thing about going to the C Hall was seeing some of the cute men over there, of course there were cute people in the crazy house. I was there!

There were four men in particular who were "fine" and crazy at the same time, literally crazy. One guy named Zack was mixed with white and Italian. He had green eyes, stood around 5'10", very hairy and muscular. He said very little to anyone. I had the girls that I was hanging around ask his name. He was the only one that ever spoke out of the four men. The other three guys didn't speak that much. One always threw up gang signs so that scared the shit out of me. He could have snapped at any moment and I didn't want to be his target.

The other guy was dark chocolate, stood around 6'2", 200 pounds solid with dreads, but he was psychotic and told one of the girls that I was hanging with when she asked his name. No lie, she said, "What's your name?" and he replied, "I'm psychotic baby, you don't want to talk to me!" Shit, we all turned around the opposite way in our chairs and the last guy out the four was only 18 years old. He had come to visit Atlanta with friends and went to a party. He said the last thing that he remembered was being checked into Anchor. Apparently, someone laced his marijuana and his alcohol and dropped him off at a police station.

******

Finally, early that morning May 8th Thursday came, and I was informed by my doctor that I was going to be released as soon as my ride arrived to pick me up. I immediately called Kevin because he was my ride home. Kevin said that he would take off work early to come get me. I told him to just come when he got off. It was no rush. Hell I had been there for nine days at that point so staying a few more hours wouldn't hurt.

I made sure I had everyone's information that I'd collected throughout my stay and I enjoyed my last day. Before long, 6 pm rolled by and my name was called over the intercom. As I hugged everyone that remained there after me, and the new comers, some cried. It felt good to know that I was loved by total perfect strangers! I learned one thing from that experience; seek help when you know you really need it!

**I was saved with GOD'S grace because I have *swag*.
(S)aved
(W)ith
(A)mazing
(G)race.**

CHAPTER 15

LOVE 'EM ALL

A lot of people wouldn't make it to the point I have in my life. I had cut many people off including family and friends. I was now living in a no-nonsense zone. My New Year's resolutions that I'd made in December of 2010 were still the same to this day. I didn't normally make them, so I choose to stick with them for life. I only had four and they were to love myself, write a book, don't worry be happy and always remember that positivity breeds positivity. I had been doing just that since that day. Now I was well on my way to finishing my second book, which at first wasn't even in my mind, let alone in my thoughts, but I wanted to be the "Face" for everything that I had run into and overcome.

I was keeping the negativity out of my life by starting with my friend Kevin and his friends, after the intervention. This was something that was pre-planned and laid-out before I even arrived at Kevin's house. Kevin was very persistent on having it right away because George said it was necessary rather than waiting any longer. I had just been released from Anchor Hospital two days earlier, following my suicide attempt. So I went on over to Kevin's for brunch knowing this was not going to go well.

At the brunch were Kevin, Quinton, George, and Kevin's nephew. Brunch was something that we had every Sunday at each other's homes and this was George's turn to host. Being George lived an hour away, he hosted at Kevin's home. George had prepared a nice brunch although he really never cooked.

He had Alfredo, baked chicken and salad. They had already eaten before I'd arrived. Everyone was responsible for bringing a bottle, so I came with mine as well. We all sat at the table in the dining room. Quinton sat to my left, George sat in front of me, Kevin sat to my right and I sat at the table with my back facing the wall. Kevin's nephew sat across from us on the couch in the living room. While I ate, they all began to say what they wanted to say. From the beginning, Kevin stated, "Please don't feel like we are ganging up on you. This is something that you need to hear to help you." I said, "Okay." As I began to eat, they began to drink. Then George started off and I really didn't like George after our little exchange of words.

******

On George's birthday that past May, George had some friends come in from out of town for his birthday party. We had all met at a restaurant/ bar called Einstein's in Midtown Atlanta. There were seven of us at the table. Everyone knows my weakness is red and yellow bone men. One of George's friends was a yellow bone. I found him attractive so I asked Kevin who he was. Kevin told me that the guy was George's friend from Chicago. He then told me to ask George about him.

I asked George in a slick way who his friend was. George said softly that they were best friends and they had hooked up years ago. He also stated that, "He got a lil dick and you could have him if I wanted to." I told George, it wasn't about the dick; it was the fact that he was a yellow bone. George never said anything else about that. We left Einstein's and went to Bull Dogs Gay Club to party. Once at Bull Dogs, we all got our life. We were drinking shots and every song came on that we liked. We tore the dance floor up as we all danced with each other.

Just like usual, someone tried to talk to me but I wasn't interested in. The closest person to me was Quinton, so I grabbed him and told the guy that he was my boyfriend. The guy walked away and we went right back into dance mode. Soon after that, another guy did the same thing. This time the closest person next to me was Kevin's friend from New York City named TJ. So I did the same thing by grabbing him and saying he was my man. TJ fell right into what I was doing and began dancing with me. It felt just like normal, like he really was my man the way it happened.

After dancing for about an hour straight, we took a break and went outside in the back of the club onto the patio. The club was about to close at that point. We were all in our friendship huddle and this guy comes along and takes my hand. He said, "Hey beautiful, can I talk to you?" The closest person next to me was George's friend from Chicago so I let go of the guys hand and grabbed George's friend. I told the guy that he was my man. The guy said okay and was still standing by us.

To play it off further, I began to hug George's friend then I began to take selfies with us holding each other as he started to wrap his arms around me. Instantly George walks off to the side and calls Kevin over. I didn't think anything of it because he had just told me I "Could" talk to his friend. After we got back to normal and after the guy walks away, Kevin calls me over as George walks away.

Kevin stated that George is feeling some type of way because I was hugged up and taking selfies with his "EX BOYFRIEND!" I'm like, "Ex-boyfriend?!" Why didn't he just tell me that from the beginning verses waiting until now that he has had a couple of drinks and all in his damn feelings?

Needless to say, it pissed me off, but saving my friendship verses talking to someone that may not even make it six months was more important and it wasn't like I was even trying to make the guy my boyfriend, let alone have sex with him. I just used him as I had done with everyone else to turn someone down. I was not the type to throw out rejection. I didn't like how rejection made me feel so I would rather say I was involved with someone instead.

Being the bigger person right after Kevin said that, I went straight to George while he was standing in front of his friend and let him know that he could have told me versus telling Kevin. I told him that I wasn't like that and I had no idea that the guy was his ex. I let him know that no dude comes between my friendships because I had gone through that with my ex before. We chalked it up as a misunderstanding and left the club cool. However, in the back of my head, I looked at him kind of different going forward.

******

The first thing that comes out of George's mouth was the situation regarding his friend from Chicago. I had just put the food in my mouth with the fork when he said, "That's bullshit." I was immediately pissed. That was an old situation that we had squashed yet he still felt some type of way about it. I knew in my heart that I was gonna be done fuckin with him that day. Basically he felt that I wasn't a good friend for talkin to someone that he'd already talked to. I didn't even have a reply, I just nodded my head and said cool, anything else you have to say; but I said it in a polite manner.

George said, "No," and I said, "Who's next?" Kevin said, "I'll go next!" Kevin began to speak. He said, "First thing I want to say is George, you did tell Sam he could talk to him though!" After that the next words came out his mouth I put my food down and stopped eating. Kevin said, "After you sucked my nephew's dick at my house I wanted to honestly beat yo ass that night!" Kevin went on to say that we were all sitting at the table and he had had the urge to reach across the table and hit my ass in the face! I didn't break my look, but in my heart right then and there, I felt like reaching across the table and whooping his ass for trying me the way had just done."

You would have thought that being we were all "*friends,*" that someone would have said something like, "Really Kevin, or come on Kevin!" But no one said anything to that effect. Instead, Quinton and George both said, "Um Hmm!" I was thinking, "Um hmm, bitch what?" So right then and there I knew our friendship was about to end as soon as I walked out the door. I was in disbelief and total awe. I felt like if I had said anything to counter their comments that they would have jumped me. I was not afraid of fighting, I was more so thinking of the fact that I would have beat the shit of them in their own house but it would have been four against one. I held my composure. Everything else out of Kevin's mouth was just bbblllaaahhh, bbblllaaahhh, bbblllaaahhhh, bbblllaaahhh, bbblllaaahhhh, to me. I was so fucking done.

To make matters worse, after he was done, I asked Quinton did he have anything to say, and this motherfucker had to the audacity to say, "I just agree with them both." I was like cool, no problem. Kevin's nephew didn't have anything to say when Kevin asked him did he have something to add. Kevin then asked me was I okay? I said, "Of course, why wouldn't I be!" With my sarcastic side stare and a slight grin. Kevin got up to get glasses for drinks, but I passed. I left about fifteen minutes later if that, and said I had to study for school being that I had missed eight days from trying to commit suicide. After I walked out that door, I never looked back. They all went from Kevin, Quinton, and George to "Who?" I was glad they didn't sugar coat anything, because I didn't like shit sweet anyway. They gave it to me just the way it was.

******

Angela had been a friend since 10th grade at Roosevelt High School. Angela and Keisha had stopped Lil Vic, Yhosogn, and Mikey D, from jumping me one day after school while walking home. Ever since that day, we had all become inseparable. However, one day in April of 2012, I decided to confide in my best friend because we told each other everything, as I do with all my best friends.

I had, had unprotected sex with someone that knew of my status. Yes, I know that it's not right to have unprotected sex with anyone because of my status however he was also HIV positive and this person knew and still wanted too. A couple of days later I had a burning sensation in my ass. I went to the doctor to find out that I had hemorrhoids due to rough sex, and I had a tear in my rectum.

I called my best friend and told her I went to the doctor and that I had a STD. I told her what the findings were and Angela was not pleased at all. She questioned me as to why I had unprotected sex and told me that I was wrong for spreading this disease. I explained to her that my partner knew of my disease and was positive too.

She still didn't care and persisted on telling me how wrong I was. After our call ended, I honestly felt some type of way.

I called my cousin Nina and Felicia and then ended up calling my sister too. I told them all the same story, and Angela's reaction to it. Everyone said the same thing; "As long as your partner knew your status, that's all that mattered!" After conversing with my family, I called Angela back that night. She didn't answer the phone, so I left a message and even sent her a text message telling her to return my phone call. She never did.

I called her numerous times in April, May and June. Throughout that entire time she was posting stats and pictures on Facebook, she even liked some of my stats. In June, I decided to give it one last try. I called Angela and to my surprise she picked up. I immediately began to tell her how I had missed her. Angela had nothing to say, she just listened to me. After I was done speaking, she spoke. She was not the nice Angela that I had known for all those years.

Angela's voice was different; it was cold with no love behind it. She stated to me that she had to re-evaluate our friendship because she didn't like the fact that I was having unprotected sex. She said I was the reason that this HIV disease continues because of people like me, furthermore she had to think about our friendship going forward. I told her I was sorry she felt that way and there was no need to think about our friendship because I was never going to call her again and just like that we hung up and never spoke to each other since.

After losing Angela's friendship, I then ended my friendship with Michial. Michial was my best friend since birth. Our grandmothers were best friends so we were raised together. Our relationship had begun to strain once he had broken up with his off and on boyfriend of many years. The last two times were just too much, even for me. Michial had caught his boyfriend cheating with some-one that he knew. In a vindictive way, Michial set his boyfriends car on fire.

Of course his boyfriend pressed charges. They were having Facebook wars daily. I got tired of seeing it and being a true friend, I decided to have a talk with Michial about his situation. I believe when someone is a true friend, they tell you exactly how it is from the heart and you all keep going. Well it didn't turn out like that for us. I told Michial that in the end he was wrong because he had cheated the entire relationship with random people and his boy-friend cheating on him with someone he had known of was just his karma.

I didn't think he would become pissed about it because he never said anything. Then one day out the clear blue sky during one of our phone conversation, Michial said, "You just think that you are better than everybody since you wrote that book!" I was blown away. Before I could even respond, Michial said he had to take the call on the other line and he would call me back. He never called me back and I would be the one ending up calling him, texting him and leaving voicemails. A couple of months passed and we went from speaking daily or every other day, to speaking once a week, to once a month, to some months passing to him not returning my phone calls at all.

It wasn't until I got in to it with Lil Vic on Facebook that Michial decided to pick up the phone and call me. By that time it was too late, four months passed and I was over him. The friendship was over to me and I didn't do second chances anymore. I can only assume that he called after the posts about Lil Vic and me because I had stated that other men from 22nd were on the DL. Michial had messed around with 1 or 2 of them but that was none of my business. It definitely was not going in my book about who he had messed with.

He was now my ex best friend, but his secrets were still safe with me, even after he made a post about me on Facebook, after he called and I didn't answer. He went on to post "People doing all this writing these books putting people business out there for what?? They didn't do shit to you for you to want to fuck up their life… For what they don't fuck with you…So why fuck with them?? What happened in the past let it stay in the past."

So of course I fed into the nonsense and clapped back with "So my Bestie since child hood is throwing out subliminal post about me. He must be scared or nervous that I am going to write about who he has been sleeping with from 22nd and Delaney! It also sounds very dumb when you're arguing from a palette in some-one else house!" After that, I left it at that, and never looked back. I learned from those two experiences that any friend that turned into an enemy has been hating since day one!

When I got into it with Lil Vic on Facebook, I learned a lot about people. I learned a lot from people who I thought were my friends but they weren't. Everyone was taking shots and posting subliminal messages. I ended up falling prey and went on the defense mode like a charging bull. I was letting people know exactly what it was and wasn't taking shots from anyone. I realized later that I had joined the circus because I was entertaining clowns. I couldn't take it back, but I didn't have to worry about the Lil Vic shit going forward.

I hadn't told anyone his name. I just said that someone from 22nd was asking me for money and head and that if they didn't stop, I would post some screen shots. He felt guilty and outed himself on my brother's page. After that, he posted death threats and I was not taking that shit lightly anymore; I was tired of it. I did the smart thing and pressed charges against him for Terroristic Threats. I did what I had to because I was not going to risk neither my life nor my freedom. I had already purchased me a gun for protection and was a license carrier. He was arrested after that for dealing cocaine to an undercover agent.

******

On my way to Minnesota passing through Gary in June of 2014, I rode through the Color Doors after leaving Evelena's. I had to pass there in order to get to the highway. While driving down the street, I drove pass a crowd of people. I rode by very slowly so I could see who was out. Being I saw people that I was cool with, I made a U turn and went back. Pulling up, I saw Angie, Zsa Zsa, Megan, Cube, and some more people. I was cool with everyone out there, I thought.

Zsa Zsa and Megan ran to the car when I rolled my tinted windows down. I had been cool with them since living in DuSable when we were teenagers. Zsa Zsa and her sister Megan and other siblings lived at the end of our building in DuSable. Zsa Zsa and Megan both hugged me through my open window. I wasn't getting out because I didn't want to stay long. Angie began walking up and she asked who was in the car. Zsa Zsa told her, "Girl this Robert!" Angie made the ugliest face and turned around holding her Ice House beer bottle in her hand. I was like, "What the fuck was that about, to Zsa Zsa?!" Zsa Zsa shrugged her shoulders and said, "I don't know!"

I was confused because Angie had been my girl since the summer when Keisha was around. We had gone way back to 1998. Now when I had first met Angie, I was going to have to whoop her ass because she kept calling me fag. I ran up on her and let her know that I was going to beat her ass. My approach is what made her get back in her body because at first she jumped out of it. After that, she was my Judy on Duty, my Ace Boom Coon. We had both slept with the same guy. Both of us had, had sex with Antonio "Coop" Cooper. As a matter fact both of us were having sex with him at the same time, she didn't care and I didn't either.

I then thought about why she was upset once I hit the highway headed for Chicago. Angie was pissed at me because I had tagged a post with her name in it about Stacy. I don't believe it was the post as much as the fact that I'd stated that Angie had known who all I had had sex with from the boys within 22nd. I understood that because she still lived in the hood and she may have felt that they might do something to her because of her knowledge. But I had apologized for the post and deleted it. We were cool after that in a phony way I guess. We were still chit chatting on Facebook here and there. But once I saw her in Gary face to face, I knew that we were not cool and that was okay because I didn't do phony people. Hell, I didn't live in Gary anyway so it was nothing.

******

I'd experienced fake friends but I knew what real friends were. Lord knows I had a slew of real friends. What would I do without my Dallas/ATL/Jersey/Minnesota family? From Tion, Damion, Miyasha, Timothy, Onesimus, Keisha, Paula, Demond, Moni, Mario, TaQuan, David, Pearl, Tha, Molly, Tyeastia, to Sharon; and of course, my girls from back home Akeka and Tika; these people were by my side more than I could ever ask for. They were my family. They were my sunshine. Without them, I truly don't know where Sam would be.

Every state I went to, I made friends who remain my friends today. I built such a strong force of friends that I was surprised how they all supported me in whatever I did. That's what we all did for each other. We stood by one another's side through thick and thin. I needed that with everything that I had gone through. I had lost two best friends that I had been friends with for a very long time and I didn't want to go through that type of hurt again. When it's all said and done, I Love 'Em All!

CHAPTER 16

I MADE IT

As of August 2012 I was matriculated at Atlanta Metropolitan State College majoring in Business Administration and expected to graduate in May of 2015, because several of my credits transferred from Indiana University Northwest located in Gary, Indiana. As of January 2015 I had been the past President of the Association Student Advocacy Group also referred to as "LGBT" (Lesbian Gay Bisexual Transgender) for almost 2 years, which I resigned from in January of 2015 in order to free up my schedule and concentrate on completing my degree. I was trying to bring awareness on campus being that Atlanta is the Black Mecca for gay and DL men.

With just three classes left I still found it to be a challenge for me in trying to focus and I was not about to jeopardize my degree. The crazy part is fourteen years ago, I was in school, and I dropped out of school because I was not approved for financial aid. Unfortunately I had not been an in state resident for one year, a prerequisite for financial aid approval. Consequently I became a prostitute to supplement my part time income as well as save money for school and living expenses. However, the money was so good that I didn't bother reenrolling there. Instead I enrolled at St. Paul Technical College in St. Paul Minnesota where I obtained my CNA (Certified Nursing Assistant) License. Initially I wanted to become a doctor but here I am today; finishing what I started but with a whole new trajectory.

I changed my major to what fits me today. My second book will be released early spring of 2015. Since September 2011 I envisioned myself being a Motivation Speaker after being inspired by some literature I'd read. I finally had the chance to speak in front of different organizations about topics in my autobiography "Eyes Without a Face." My very first speaking engagement was in Boston, Massachusetts on November 2, 2013 at a Domestic Violence Awareness Convention. Ironically that was 3 years to the day that I was robbed, beaten and almost car jack resulting from being a victim in a Domestic Violent relationship. I was hand selected and flown out by Debbie Chambers. We met from a mutual friend on Facebook named Colleen Williams. We all shared something in common; we'd all been victims of abuse in some way and all had become close friends.

This was something that I had dreamed of doing; speaking in front of an audience listening to me telling my story. I flew in on Delta one Friday evening. The feeling was awesome and I truly am grateful for it. Once I arrived in Boston, Debbie and Colleen picked me up from the airport. Prior to that we'd all been connected on Facebook and then on the phone. I felt like I'd known them for many years however meeting them in person seemed like I was meeting my friends for the very first time as we embraced each other in a group hug. We had been speaking on Facebook for almost a year before we met.

We drove around the city and then stopped at the Farmers Market to get dinner. I spent the night at Debbie's house. We stayed up and ate our food, shared our stories and discussed how tomorrow would play out. This was Debbie's convention that she had been having for years. The mission was "Empowering Children and Surviving Sexual Abuse." I found her to be a strong woman who had faced so much and she made it through it all. I was honored that she'd offered me the opportunity to share my story at her event.

The next morning we woke up at 6 am and started getting ready. Debbie had to make a lot of runs to ensure everything would go smoothly. She delegated some things to other people but took on the more important things herself. Debbie asked if I was nervous. I told her yes because this would be my first engagement in front of a large crowd. I'd done numerous radio interviews but no one was ever this close in my face. The most powerful face-to-face video that I had done was an interview Walter Hampton II, who has his own online internet show. I'd disclosed my HIV status and didn't even realize it until after I watched the video on YouTube. I would actually have a live audience this time. Debbie told me that everything was going to be alright and I would present my story just fine, to just be myself and tell the story exactly how I wanted to because it was my story.

Once we arrived at the church where the convention was held, my nervousness slowly diminishing. I met people from all walks of life. There was no color barrier, men and women young and some old. No one knew that I was the Keynote Speaker until I was announced. We all had breakfast and then the convention began.

Debbie had her schedule down pat; I was second to the last to go on stage. While listening to each of the speakers share their stories,

I was struck by the similarities in a life of abuse with one striking difference, I was the only man waiting to share. The sounds of the voices around me seemed to fade as my mind was drawn back to years of pain and abuse from my own past. I'd worked hard to keep my composure and now, moments before my introduction, I felt tears roll down my cheeks as a lifetime of emotions were about to overtake the moment. Then out of nowhere came thoughts of my mother and as Debbie was introducing me all I could think of was how I wished my mother were here. I felt an urge to tell her that I loved her so much and I wanted her to know that I didn't blame her for what had happened to me. The sudden thunder of applause brought me back to the moment as Debbie called my name.

Approaching the podium, I looked out and saw nothing but people hurt from their past. I saw faces of desperation as to how do I go on from what happened. I had my speech prepared. After I had been speaking for a while I observed people crying and covering their mouths, at that point I knew I had their undivided attention. In return, while reading my pain made tears flow from my own eyes. I had rehearsed for that moment to keep from crying by telling the story as if it were someone else's story.

Unfortunately, while telling my story, I was actually reliving the incidents as though they were happening in real time, but the most amazing thing happened as I delivered the words I had written, the anger was gone. I was telling my story from someone who was hurt and had start wishing that others understood the pain caused from those actions. When I was done speaking, the crowd gave me a standing ovation, which felt refreshing. I was the only male that spoke at the event and I knew that event was first of many to come. Once I sat back down and the last person went on, all the authors began to sell their books. I sold every single book that I took with me. If I had paid for that trip, I could have paid for it twice with the money I made from my books sales. After that, I was rushed back to the airport by Debbie and Colleen because I was about to miss my flight. We said our good byes and I thanked them again for the opportunity.

My second event was held in July of 2014 at the Georgia International Congress Center in College Park, Georgia. I spoke at the Georgia PTA Summit for their 100th Year Anniversary. I was working with Myron Schippers and Richard "Rajheem" Williams of Lezah Development Group, LLC on getting my first book "Eyes Without a Face" to the next level. They had pushed for many things and this engagement was first of many to come which I'd be booked as the Keynote Speaker. Surprisingly when I spoke at the PTA Summit I wasn't nervous at all because I realized that this is my calling. I was asked to speak about the impact of Bullying and Abuse on people. I was speaking to children, teens, young adults and parents, my target audience.

The feeling of being up at the podium felt amazing because I was fulfilling my passion. Once again, I practiced telling this story from a third person point of view. After I was finished speaking, Rajheem began asking me questions. I was okay at first until he asked me, "Samuel, if you could, what would you change?" I thought about it for a second and then the tears came pouring out, so I had to pause before responding. I had a "Valley Experience." A valley experience consists of 3 things Unavoidable, Unpredictable and Unscheduled. The Shepherd and goodness and mercy are the two things you need in order to walk through the valley. Most of the things that happened to me and others were unavoidable, unpredictable and unscheduled. However the Shepherd and goodness and mercy brought us through. My valley was just a little different from others. I replied, "If I had to change anything, I wouldn't! Everything that happened to me was meant to happen to me. It made me the person that I am today and it shaped my character and I will forever be grateful for it."

******

My trip back to Minnesota for my twin niece's graduation was a trip to remember. I experienced both good and bad but the memories were priceless. I set out on my trip on Sunday June 1st at midnight. This would be the second time that I made the twenty-hour drive to Minnesota alone, I was a road warrior so it didn't bother me. As long as I had my music I was always ready for a road trip. I decided along the way that I would stop in certain cities to visits my friends and family that I hadn't seen in a while. I was really in a hugging mood being that the month before I was released from Anchor Hospital for trying to kill myself. A lot of my family and friends already knew so I didn't have to explain anything really except "why" if they had asked.

The first placed I stopped after ten hours was in Indianapolis at Moon's house. At 9 am I was stuck in traffic prior to arriving, my feet hurt and my body ached, but I was wide awake and wired from all the coffee and Red Bulls. Moon had just got off work and was waiting on me. I had called him while I was on the road to let him know that I would be stopping by. My cousin D'Andre was over at Moon's house waiting on me also, they were best friends.

Moon was standing outside when I pulled up because I had called him soon as I exited the highway by his house. We embraced each other, as I hadn't seen Moon in over five years. It felt good to see someone that I loved so much and looked up too. Moon was doing real good for himself, he had a job, a crib and a car.

"WURK bitch!" I said, while going into his house. My cousin rolled up a couple blunts and we smoked and talked. My other cousin Antawyone called and wanted to meet up before I left. After we finished smoking, D'Andre and I rode to meet Antawyone at Cracker Barrel. We all sat down and ate breakfast and caught up before I headed back out. Antawyone didn't even know that D'Andre was his cousin.

Antawyone is Uncle Kenny's son and we are the same age but he wasn't raised around us. None of us had met Antawyone until Christmas in 1994 at Grandma Hazel's house. His mom had finally bought him over while they visited family in Gary. He and his mom lived in Milwaukee. Antawyone became my favorite boy cousin other than Demetruis. After we all ate, we hugged and promised to keep in touch. D'Andre and I went back to Moon's and I passed out before I hit the highway for Chicago.

I woke up and it was almost 2 O'clock in the afternoon. I figured I should leave if I didn't want to get stuck in Chicago's rush hour traffic. While I was riding to Chicago, I decided to stop in Gary. I figured being that I was going to hit traffic I may as well stop. Before I could get out of Merrillville good enough, traffic was backed up. I called my cousin Evelena and told her to meet me at her house. When I pulled up about forty-five minutes later, Evelena was waiting for me. My mom pulled up just as I was hugging Evelena.

Of course I was happy to see my mom. I hadn't seen her since she sent for me to come to Minnesota for Thanksgiving in November of 2012. I think everyone that has been through it with their parents still love them till the end. No matter what my mother and I had gone through, I still loved her. No matter all the bad that she had done to me, I still wanted that mother-son relationship. I loved my mother and yearned for her love daily, but my mother still felt some type of way about my book.

My mother was still sitting in her car blasting the radio so I went over to give her a hug after I hugged Evelena. Hell I had just tried to commit suicide. I wanted a hug from every damn body. I was crying for love and acceptance still at the age of 35 years old. My mother pulled away from me and said she didn't want a hug from me because I had endangered her life by things I wrote about concerning her in my book. She said that now people were out to kill her so I looked at her crazy as hell. Just when that happened, my cousin Bernice and my Aunt Denise pulled up. Bernice is my cousins Kim and Black Black mother. I love me some Bernice. Denise is my mom's oldest sister. It was so funny because when I was a child Aunt Denise and I didn't get along, but now, she's one of my favorite aunts and we talked all the time on the phone. We all hugged each other right away. They had hugged me so tight that it brought tears to my eyes.

I eventually turned back and told my mom that I loved her with all my heart. I also told her that the book wasn't to bash her. I was trying to explain to her that the book was like a guide to other mothers who have gone through something similar with their children; especially if they had a gay child. I also told her that no one was out to kill her because of my book. It would have been me if anything that they wanted to kill. That was the last time that my mother and I spoke to each other.

Evelena and I sat in my car and I rolled a blunt, smoked and made a singing video before I got right back on the highway. I was about the hit the city of Chi town where I was going to meet Lucciano since I'd be staying at his house over night before heading to my final destination, Minnesota. The twin's graduation was that

Wednesday at 3 pm, so I was leaving at 8 am. It would only be a six hour drive, but five the way I drove. Lucciano and I hit the streets that night and just hung out, it was nice being around him. On our way to turn in for the night, we stopped at Maxwell's Restaurant and got that famous polish sausage that Price had turned me on to.

We got our food and headed back to his house, ate and we passed out. The next morning I woke up right on schedule. I showered and was headed to pick up Keisha. She was Price's auntie who was visiting Chicago to attend a family member's funeral. She and I still remained friends after Price and I had split up. We had planned on her riding back to Minnesota with me instead of catching the bus with her sons. I called Keisha, Price's aunt, to tell her that I was on my way and she informed me that she was at her sister's house who is also Price's mother.

Right when I pulled up, she called and said, "Price is here, do you want us to just come down or do you want to come up?" I told her I would come up; I didn't care if Price was there or not. Keisha's oldest son opened the door and I gave him a hug. He said, "Wow, Sam I haven't seen you in forever!" It made me smile because he still remembered me. He was only five years old when Price and I spilt and now he was 10 years old. I walked into the house and the first person sitting by the door I saw was Price. I was not even bothered at all. He said, "Hey Sam." I said, "Hey, Price," and then his mom came and hugged me right away. Even though I still harbored some feelings toward his mom, I didn't allow that to show. I felt some type of way because when Price and I broke up, she felt that I should have left him with some of the furniture rather than taking it all but I felt totally opposite. He didn't buy shit and you knew he was cheating too. *REALLY!!??* I thought.

But that was neither here nor there. It was in the past so I went on like nothing happened and nothing bothered me. I sat down and we all chatted for a minute. I sat across from Price and Keisha, the boys and Price's mom sat next to me on the couch toward my left. Price was directly in front of me but my eyes stayed on them. I noticed him in my peripheral looking at me the entire time. After a few minutes of entertaining them, I was like, "We have to go because I'm on a time schedule." Keisha said her goodbyes to her family and I hugged everyone and said goodbye too. I didn't hug Price but said goodbye to him.

What a coincidence that he left the same times as me. Hmmm? Keisha and I packed her bags into my car and Price who was parked directly in front of my car was sure to let me see him leave before me because he either wanted me to see that he was driving someone else's car or he wanted to see mine since it was a new one; again! To be honest I think he wanted me to see the car though but I was unbothered. I was in a relationship and couldn't have cared less about him. I was in love and nothing he could have done or said would have changed that. We stopped communicating after he read the letter and book that I sent him. This is what I wrote to Price...

******

Dear Price,

First off, I want to say "Thank you." Job well done! By the time you finish reading this letter, you'll understand why I say thank you in advance. Some people are hurting so bad; you have to do more than preach a message to them. You have to be a message to them. So this is my message to you.

I can't believe that I actually have to write this versus calling you but hey, it is what it is. I tried to befriend you, but unfortunately every time we seem to get back close, something comes along. This last time was just too much. When you tell the people that you're about to fuck about your life, DO NOT INCLUDE ME IN IT. Change my name. Hence, I changed yours. I don't do that let me show you him shit. If I did, they wouldn't believe that you're even my type. Not being rude, just being honest. Stop showing my FB page. And tell Tone Smart Ass to stop posting shit on my Fan Page. Or he may be you being that he uses your picture. SMH... I honestly and with all my heart, do not hate you, nor have any ill will feeling towards you. As much as I should, I don't! I don't even wish you any type of harm the way you wished on me.

Things have to happen for a reason. And now looking back, I'm glad everything did. You see, right from the beginning, I kept coming back; I kept trying to win your heart. GOD said, "Once He closes a door, stop pulling on it to open again." I never understood that quote as much as I do today. I wanted you after all the cheating you did. I knew every time, but all along I turned a blind eye. I didn't want to believe what was right in front of my very own eyes. Sadly, all the writings had already been written on the wall.

There were just so many people that you screwed. And I do mean literally screwed one way or another. You are a conartist! You may or may not think so, but you are. Living in your TRUTH is the best way to live. Being honest with people is the best way to get you further. I'll explain that later in this letter. You messed over a number of people. I pray that you don't go on hurting people to make yourself feel good, or to get what you want. It's not worth it in the end.

You had your mom believing the worst about me, and I'm quite sure she believes the worst about others also. All because of the lies you told her and again, that's sad. I can't even blame your parents for the way you are. I blame you. No one should ever have to take the blame of someone so evil. I learned so much about liars. I've learned that the most dangerous liars are those who think they are telling the truth. The prettiest person at that time, turned out to be a total monster. Looking at you today, you resemble more of that monster. You don't even look the same.

I had unblocked you, after I had prayed for you for about seven months. That's how long you had been blocked. I prayed for your health and wealth. I prayed that what you did to me, you wouldn't do to others. I prayed this prayer, because that's what you do when you love someone. I DON'T LOVE YOU LIKE THAT! I DON'T WANT TO BE WITH YOU LIKE THAT! I love you because of the good times we shared. I love you because I never thought I could fall in love with someone who loved me, just as much as I loved them. Oh but was I so wrong. You didn't love me. You loved my money, my material things, and the things that I could do for you. And that's sad too.

When I say you don't even look the same, I am referring to how KARMA has taken its course. Have you looked in the mirror lately?! When I see the picture of you and the boys, when Keisha came to visit, I didn't recognize you at all. It took for someone to call me and say, "Have you seen your husband's picture with Keisha?!" You know some of my family is still friends with your family on FB. I said, "Yes, and that's not Price, that's one of Keisha's friend's. I was told to go back and look again. So I went back and I looked again. I had scrolled right past this picture the first time I saw it.

This time, I looked long and hard. I tried to see you. I tried to see what I saw before. But after it came to light, it was you in the picture. I tell you, KARMA came back in a way that you would have never thought. You look really bad. Really bad! You look old and sick. I'm not trying to be mean by far, nor throw any shade. It's just crazy because we all know that KARMA comes back in 100 fold. You can't just go by life fucking over people, and not expect anything to go wrong. Sometimes KARMA may not come to you, but come to a loved one. In your case, KARMA took your "Pretty Boy" status away, and left you looking like you had got a hold to some bad crack. I'm sorry, but in my Future voice, "I'm Just Being Honest!"

What you had done to me, in some people's eyes would be unforgettable. Instead, I have to forgive you. I took that ass whooping like a champ. I almost lost my life for it, but I am still alive today, and not to mention, I look FABULOUS after all the surgeries! I don't even blame you fully. I have to take some blame myself. I went back. I was asking for something to happen knowing damn well, you had already slept with as many people as you could in Dallas. It was like a race for you to see how many people you could screw. Or it was a race to see how many you could get from another state.

I had to go through all of that to get to where I am today. Today, I am more than elated. I've only had two relationships, and one little fling, that lasted a good couple months. Everyone that I had dealt with, we all separated on a positive note. The best of friends is what we call it. Who buys their EX a new car?! My ex!!! In fact, the way that you kept saying, "Nothing is guaranteed Sam, and if we don't make it, we could at least still be friends!" Well that's just what happened for me, and my first relationship that lasted over a year, and my little fling that lasted a couple of months. And I'm going on two years with my second relationship. Everything happens for a reason!

If you had never cheated, broken up with me, stole my things, and got me robbed, and nearly killed, I would have never gotten into these relationships with people who truly loves me with all their heart, replaced everything that was taken 1,000 fold, and much more. Not to mention that I crawled through the burning lake of fire and walked through shit, just to come out smiling like a bed of roses, and feeling FILTHY FUCKING RICH!!! HA.....Yes, I had to laugh at that one too; but only because it's so true. You see what you meant for the bad, GOD meant for the good. No one can hurt his child and get away with it. NO ONE! What's meant for me is only for me! My dreams and my visions are mine saith the LORD! Vengeance as well!!

This letter was simply written to you, to ask for a divorce. That's it, that's all. I stayed by my husband when he had nothing. I stayed by my husband after he cheated. I stayed by my husband after he received the voicemail from Lucciano. In Lucciano's own words, "I gave you something so bad, it will make you sick to your damn stomach!" Yes, we both heard that! I stayed by my husband after he contracted Syphilis. We weren't having sex, that's why I didn't get it. Then you turned around and got it again, and this nicca said, "It came back!" REALLY DUDE?! (LMAO) I stood by my husband, after you got a job at Wells Fargo, and listed your mother on your life insurance policy for 100%! I stood by you, after you stayed with Samar for four days, and thought nothing was wrong with it. I stayed by my husband's side, after he let Samar fuck him in his ass, and you came home to soak your ass, because you were in pain on the 3rd day, all the while I washed your back knowing my husband had just been fucked!

Through it all, I stood by my husband's side because that's what a real husband would do. I would have died for you. Thank GOD I didn't have too, because I would later learn that you would have had me killed if the cards fell right. And that's sad. However, breakups hurt, but losing someone who doesn't respect and appreciate you is actually a gain, and not a loss.

But that's neither here, nor there. It's in the past and I have let it go. Now back to the divorce. Now that true, real love, has found me, I want it! That's all I ever wanted. Now that I have it, I can't go further with it, except for having a ceremony, and you know I can't go out like that! You know me; I want the whole damn shebang. I want this to be better than the $25,000.00 dollar wedding that we had. We want something so beautiful, that no one would believe it. We can have that too, but I need a divorce in order for this dream to come true. You should be happy right now. You're working, have a crib, and whatever else. You never wanted me, and now you can be totally free. No strings attached. NSA...HA HA HA...Isn't that how you like things anyway?! No pun!

Anyways, AGAIN, you have to file. Georgia does not recognize Gay Marriage, but Illinois does. I spoke with a lawyer there. Now that you have a job, I could file, and collect alimony. I would apply for this "IF" I have to come there, and do all the work myself. But I will walk away gracefully, if you would just apply; or allow me to help you apply, so everything is filled out correctly. I want to be happy with who's happy with me. There is no need to negotiate happiness, when we already compromise. That's something that you couldn't learn.

I thank you for the run we had, although we know that wasn't real. That took a long time for me to realize, but I do know now. You never loved me, and I am honestly okay with that. I can live with it. I have been living with it for seven years already (three years that we were together, and the four years that we have been apart). I got over it, and it feels great to walk away with the memories of the good times that we did have. We did have many, but unfortunately, that was lie too. Now, today, I just want to be free, and be with the person who honestly loves me. You see, sometimes you just have to erase the messages, delete the numbers and move on. You don't have to forget who that person was to you; you just have to accept that they aren't that person anymore.

Samuel P. Holloway III

April 21, 2014 EXACTLY 4 YEARS TO THE DAY OF WHEN WE PARTED WAYS

******

Keisha and I hit the highway around 9 am, there was little traffic so we were cruising. Soon as we got to Elmhurst, Illinois, I caught a flat tire. We weren't even two hours from the city and now we were stranded. I say stranded because I couldn't change a flat and I had never changed a flat tire in my life. Thank GOD for Roadside Assistance. It was unbelievable because I kept having dreams of being stranded in Gary. I would tell my cousins and sister that I kept dreaming of my car breaking down, someone stealing it and it being towed away while I was in Gary during my dreams, and here it was actually happening. I was so terrified but relieved at the same time because I was not in Gary.

While Keisha, the boys and I were riding on the highway, a motorist on the side of us kept waving their hands and blowing their horn at us, to whom I paid no attention to because we were talking and singing. I only noticed them when they pulled from on the left side of us and got in front and pressed on their brakes. I was like, "What the fuck!" They then pulled back on the on my side and rolled down their windows. I assumed they were a married couple with children. The lady yelled out as I rolled down my window, and screamed, "Your tire is going to blow if you keep driving, you have a flat!" I guess because we were so deep in our conversation and songs that we didn't even notice. I nearly lost my mind within five seconds. Luckily, there was a gas station not even five hundred feet from where we were. I pulled off on the exit and they pulled off too. I got out and looked and I sure did have a flat. The front tire on the passenger side was completely deflated. I would have never expected to be having a flat tire because I had special tires on the car, which were brand new and can be driven a great distance even when deflated. The man in the truck came over and wanted to help change the tire. I told him I didn't have a spare because the 2013 Kia does not come with a spare, but an air pump instead! I called Roadside Assistance and they said it would be at least an hour before they arrived.

I was getting paranoid because my niece's graduation was scheduled for 3 pm and it was already 11 am. I had only four hours to make it to Minnesota and I knew I was going to be late. Roadside Assistance didn't arrive until noon. The driver told me that he could not tow the car because I had passengers but that the Kia dealership was only fifteen minutes away and if I drove slowly I could make it. I was beyond pissed because I just sat there and wasted an hour already, so we made that slow drive to the dealership. I had called ahead of time so they would be ready for us when we arrived. As soon as we arrived they had me on priority and took the car into service, it was repaired within thirty minutes and we were on our way. The only problem was by that time, it was almost 1pm and I knew I was not going to make it on time.

I ended up calling my niece's cell phones to let them know what had happened. They didn't answer because they were in rehearsal. I then called their mom, Rachel, to let her know and I was almost in tears. This was a very sentimental moment for me to see my nieces graduate and I was not going to be there. Rachel told me it was okay and that things happen. We hung up and a few minutes later the twins called me on speakerphone. They both were like, "Uncle Sam, it's okay if you can't make it, as long as you come to see us is all that matters." I loved my girls; they knew the right words to say to cheer me up. I put the petal to the metal and punched it. I at least wanted to be outside when they came out of the ceremony.

We arrived in Minnesota right at 5 pm. Keisha lived right around the corner from my nieces and where the graduation was taking place. After I dropped Keisha and the boys off, I B-lined to the ceremony. Sure enough, I had missed it and pulled up right as they were walking out; I could have died. My nieces called me right away to see where I was. I told them I was right next door at the gas station and they came right over. We all hugged so hard and cried. I loved them just like they were my children. I had them from when they were three until seven years old and regularly after that. This was the day that I had waited on and I had missed it.

I gave them their gifts, which was a card with $100 in them each. Rachel told the girls they could go with me being that I was leaving the next morning. Summer school had started on June 2nd but I was missing the first week because I had to see my babies walk across that stage. I had already emailed my Professors before I left and got their approval. The twins came back with me over Felicia's house. Tonya met up with me so I could get little Zadie too. I had all my brother's kids with me just like old times. I had wished that I could bring them back to Atlanta with me, but the twins were going off to the Army to pursue their careers in Chemical Biological Radiological and Nuclear Specialists (CBRN Specialists). My babies knew what they wanted to be and they both were going to be the same thing. I thought that was very special since they are twins.

My family and some friends met over Felicia's like usual for round table. Everyone from Kim, Lisa, Delores, my brother and the kids were there. Most of the kids were now young adults and had just graduated. I had three other little cousins that were the same age as the twins that graduated from high school. The next day I took everyone home and went to visit my grandmother, Aunt Sylvia, cousins Nikki and her wife Keysha. Everyone else I missed because they were at work. Seeing my grandmother made me cry. I loved my grandmother and my grandmother loved me. My grandmother told me, "Keep doing what you are doing because you are helping somebody baby" and I broke down crying and she just hugged me. After seeing my grandmother, I got right back on the highway by noon.

I had done a whole turn around trip. I had left on Sunday at midnight, which was actually Monday morning. I had arrived in Minnesota on Wednesday and was now headed back to Chicago so I could be back at home in Atlanta by Friday. I ate up those six hours on the way to Chicago very quickly. I didn't speed because police were everywhere on the road. I made it to city by 6 pm though. I went to meet up with my cousins first before I went to Lucciano's. I would be meeting them for the first time in my life. They're my cousins on my maternal grandfather's side. We all had been talking on Facebook for some time now.

I had so much family in Chicago that I had never met. I arrived at Randy's house and from there we rode to his mom's where several other unfamiliar cousins were gathered. Randy and I looked just alike. It was very rare to admit that someone looked like me but I had to realize our genes were strong and I had a couple of cousins that resembled me or I resembled them. When we arrived Randy's mom, his sister Erica along with her son and her nephew were already there. We all chit chatted and snapped a few pictures and I left after only a short time. All of my visits were short because I was trying to get back to Atlanta.

I left there and met up with Lucciano and we went to his aunt's house so I could change clothes. We had planned to go out with Arius, Marcel, Andrew and Donald but we had one too many shots and I was too wasted. I knew my limit but I was being an asshole. We were on our way to the club and I was speeding on the highway. Everyone kept telling me to slow down but I thought I had it. All of a sudden, this lady driving about 100 mph came speeding behind me, crossed over right in front of me, and to avoid rear-ending her car, I swerved and lost control of my car. I hit the curb and spun out. Once I gained control of the car I pulled to the side of the roadway and noticed that the rear passenger side tire had blown out. There I was again, stranded in Chicago in the middle of the fucking night. This damn dream had come true again. It was too late to get a new tire so we left my car parked off the exit ramp on 87th Ave and took the tire off and put in the trunk of Andrews car.

I couldn't sleep at all because I felt my car was going to get stolen, towed or ticketed because it was parked in a permit parking area only. We all got up early that next morning and drove around trying to find a tire to fit my car. I called the Kia dealership that was in downtown Chicago, but they said they would have to special order the tire and it would not be there until Monday morning. Oh that was some bullshit and I was not waiting nor staying in Chicago that long, plus I had to back go to school. We drove around to different tire shops until we found one that would fit my car. We finally found one that wasn't the same name brand, but it was the same size. They mounted the tire to the rim and I paid $50 and we were on our way. Once Lucciano and Andrew changed the tire, I got my ass on the highway right away. I felt like I could not stay in Chicago anymore because I didn't want anything else bad to happen. I had left Chicago headed for Indianapolis.

I left there at 2 pm and arrived in Gary by 3 pm. I had to get my sweet potato pies from Akeka before I went back home. They were my favorite and she placed an order from her friend or mom every time I came to town. Akeka was my girl from back in DuSable; we went way back. We considered each other brother and sister and I had told her everything. Ironically she was one of many that knew about all the DL men that I had slept with. As teenagers, we didn't think of it as me being molested because we were too young to understand although a lot of people had said that I kept it on the low do to the fact that I'd slept with the DL men, but many girls that I was cool with knew. They didn't need to say anything to prove a point to anyone because it was between us.

We had taken some pictures of each other and together and I took pictures with her son. He was my baby in my head and was so adorable. I gave him a pop sickle and I ate one too so he'd let me hold him because he was spoiled rotten. Before I stopped at Akeka's, I ran into Lil Vic who'd seen me driving and flagged me down. We both pulled over, got out and I went in for the normal routine straight hug with one arm but he hugged me differently, in a way that made me pull back from him and say, "What the fuck was that?!" Lil Vic had hugged me like he was hugging a girl, which threw me for a loop. He laughed and started asking for money after he asked how I was doing. I cut that visit short and headed to Akeka's.

I left Akeka's headed for Indianapolis right after that. I arrived there about 8 pm because of traffic and accidents along the way. Moon was off that Thursday and was expecting me. We got high, ate and talked about old times and then passed out afterwards. I woke up that next morning at 5 am and got ready to hit the highway back to Atlanta. I was not ready for this ten to eleven hour drive. I was tired of the highway at that point but I had to do it. The entire ride back, I sang every song that came on the satellite and the songs from the CD's I brought. I made it back to Atlanta by 5 pm and sat in traffic for almost two damn hours before I made it home. When I walked in the door, I showered and got in the bed and didn't wake up until the next day. I was exhausted.

******

In March of 2013, I met #14. I was still trying to get back with #26 when I met #14. Everyone knows I never post pictures or post the name of anyone that I was dating. I had a thing about that because if it didn't work, I didn't want to be having my Facebook timeline filled with names of different dudes. So, instead of doing that, I posted a number that represented their birthdays. I've only had two numbers since moving to Atlanta in December of 2010. I also had a fling that didn't make it three months, so there was no number to represent him. The ironic part is that every person that I dated were Leos (Zodiac Sign). #26's Birthday is July 26th, #14's birthday is August 14th and Price's is August 3rd.

I loved them all but the love was only reciprocated by #'s 26 and 14. #14 And I dated for a little over a year, which was a great relationship probably because we had so much in common. Just like every man that I promised myself that I would date had to have the three C's, Car, Crib, and Career. I didn't want anything less being that Price came with nothing. I was not taking care of another grown ass man. #14 Owned a landscaping company and even had a contract with the college that I was attending. He was very generous with his money, he didn't mind sharing nor making sure I was well taken care of. Our relationship hit a bump in August when #26 came into town to visit and stopped by our house to say hello.

However, the day before #26 left, I had taken my car to the Kia Dealership to have a tune up done and buy new tires. With all the road trips I had taken, my tires had worn out quickly. #26 met me at the dealership because he wanted to have lunch before he went back to NYC. While we were at the dealership waiting in the waiting area for my car to be serviced the agent came out and said there were a couple of issues that needed to be addressed right away. The total cost was about $2,500.00. #26's Brother is the Assistant Manager at the dealership. #26 Went in the office and spoke with his brother while I looked at cars. #26 Came out and said pick a car! I was flabbergasted. Pick a car I said?! Are you serious?

#26 Said, "Although we are not together, you should have anything that you want." I owned the 2011 Kia, so we put that down and #26 added a few more thousand dollars. I walked out the dealership with a brand new 2013 fully loaded Kia Optima Sport for the dirt. I loved my new car with all the fixings. #26 Continued to be a blessing despite us not being together. I was angrier at myself now more than ever for cheating on him. The saying that Price used to say to me was so true right now. Price always told me, "You never miss what you have until it's gone." Now I was missing what I had because he was gone and in a relationship.

I arrived at home, #14 saw the new car when I pulled up, he already knew beforehand that I was bringing the new car home because I called and informed him that #26 was able to get me a deal I couldn't refuse and that I'll be late getting home. He wanted me to take it back and allow him to purchase me a vehicle instead but I told him it wasn't that serious. #14 Forbade me to have any contact with #26 going forward. I told him that he was out of his rabbit ass mind and that would never happen. I told him I'd rather lose him than lose #26, but our relationship meant a lot to me I so didn't want to lose it.

We continued our relationship but I believed he had trust issues. I never had any problems with him except one; he was an alcoholic. He wasn't abusive towards me, but he was abusive towards himself, he would drink just to be drinking and had got so drunk one day that he fell off the couch. On New Year's 2014, Kevin hosted a party at his house. #14 Was already drunk before we left home which was embarrassing. His speech was slurred, he couldn't walk without staggering and stumbling and he reeked of alcohol. Right after midnight we had to leave because he was getting smart with people for no reason, spilling his drink that he insisted on having and fell off a chair at Kevin's house. I was too embarrassed and was quite done with the situation and him all together. We continued dating until September of 2014 following an ultimatum I gave him in August; either go to rehab or we are done. He refused saying that "Only alcoholics go to rehab." I decided that 9 months of hell was enough so I gave him the boot. I will always love him because he's been there for me and still is today but we can't be together.

I was content with life, nothing could stop me. I was back to myself again and I was happy. I had my braces and my smile. I would have to have the braces in my mouth for another two years and was going to have them tightened every six weeks. At first it seemed cool however as time progressed I truly despised going to see the Orthodontist. It kept bringing back the memories of why I was there in the first place but the saying is true, "Time heals all wounds!" I had to go through that valley and I was humbled for the experience.

My best friend Onsemious is my life and he's straight too! I looked at him like my younger brother. He didn't judge me and he understood me. We had many similarities. He was on his venture to start a nonprofit youth organization to help the male youth in his community. He was holding events to help young boys accomplish the mission of earning their first jobs by having resume builder seminars. His family owned some of the soul food restaurants here in Atlanta and he took advantage of that by hiring the youth.

I was proud of him for trying to make a positive impact within his community. His parents and family were loving and acceptable, I loved them all and they loved me too. Onsemious reminded me of my little play brother BJ from back home in Minneapolis. He was just like him in every way. Onsemious was Heaven sent, I learned Atlanta because of him. The only problem that I had with Onsemious is he kept stealing my damn lighters.

******

It was November 2014 and I was approaching the final pages of this book after three years diligent work and going to school at the same time. Yes it was a challenge but once I put my mind to something I will see it through regardless how long it takes. In my opinion studying and writing the book was a huge task but I decided that I'd do it, now look at me. Thanksgiving was right around the corner and all my friends were coming back into town to have Thanksgiving dinner at my house. After that, the next event was my birthday, which was right around the corner in December and my bestie Timothy had already planned a road trip to Miami. I couldn't have asked for anything more. The feeling was great!

Children don't have voices many times; especially young children, but they do grow up. "I've decided when life throws me lemons, I'm going to make brownies out of them and leave the world wondering how the fuck I did it! I'm living a POSITIVE life in all aspects!"

~ Samuel P. Holloway III

I've Learned It's Never The End
So We Will Just Say, Until Next Time...

Some will be shocked...
Some will be surprised....
Some will be sad....
Some will mad....
Some will be hurt....
And some will be encouraged....
But guess what, at the end of the day,
It is what it is!
Now put my shoes on...If you can fit them!

The Strength of My Body

By Shantell Floyd

As my mind drifts off to memories,
I see demons attacking trying to take over my body
Starting from the ages of 10-12
My mother beat me and my brother constantly punched at my body
While my body was being used as a punching bag
I became scared of dark eyes from a man I was supposed to call dad
Molested at 8-10 my body was something he should have never had
As he dangled my body over a body of water
He said if I ever told anybody
No one will find me, not even my father
At 10 male Cousins took advantage of me
Touching my body anyway they pleased
At 12 I started having sex with brother's close friends
They all wanted my body and they were all men
At 14 years old running through the streets,
Hot medal pierced through my body I felt the heat
Blood poured from my right side of my back
As I heard the loud sounds of the gun
Moving my legs as my body flew I still had to run
Raped at the age of 22 my body was violated in my own bedroom
To confirm he would ditch my body
if I told anyone he sliced my arm before he left
Vivid pictures going through my mind as history was repeating it self
I was 32 when I seen the rage of a man my husband had an affair with
Hating me to my soul he convinces his friends I was a sweet lick
They robbed me in the back seat of my car
while repeatedly hitting me in the head
Dumping my body leaving me for dead
My body had been attacked by demons all my life
but never could they take me

If I hadn't suffered enough the devil still wasn't through with me
So he hit me with a disease called HIV
My body was molested, my body was beaten, my body was shot,
but my body was never defeated
Thank God I don't look like what the demons had done to me
I am a living witness that GOD is good because I'm here at 33
Because I was broken into pieces but I was mended together
The demons might have attacked my body but my soul the LORD has
FOREVER...

A Stumbling Place

By Shantell Floyd

I SPENT MANY YEARS IN A STUMBLING PLACE

20 years in a cell of pain from being caged away
By my memories
Sitting and stuck in this jail called reality

Reality from being taunted by 10 men who used me
Mentally abused me
By teaching me how to be sexually

I SPENT MANY YEARS IN A STUMBLING PLACE

A place with these 10 grown men
Which 7 were friends of my brother he would call
2 were brothers 1 was the man of my mother
It was he who started it all

8 years old my innocents being taken away from me
Followed by 7 more years being molested
My mind spent 20 years in a cell

I SPENT MANY YEARS IN A STUMBLING PLACE

These grown men who
Are known as gang bangers, drug dealers, and killers had me doing
Grown people things
All this going on while I was only a pre-teen

Put a gun to my head
And said if I told anyone I was dead

Believing his eyes because I saw his rage
So many years I kept my mouth closed not telling a soul
Only becoming their sex slave

I SPENT MANY YEARS IN A STUMBLING PLACE

I fell in love with one of my molesters who was a red bone
Because he was sensual
More caring and filled me with satisfaction
While the dark skin men had me
Doing nasty things making me feel disgusting but money and gifts
speaks
Louder than actions

Now I have a complex only dating light skin men
Dark skin ones don't attract me
So abused made me so confused with my faith at 18

I SPENT MANY YEARS IN A STUMBLING PLACE

I have been molested, bullied, raped, and beaten to the point
Where I almost met death
Walking you through my journey of life I realize the only one who was
There was GOD and myself

When I step into the shower the tears start rolling as GOD washes
away my pain
It's HE I give all glory
Almost meeting death no longer feared no man so I told my story

Knowing I can save a life by writing *"Eyes Without A Face"*
I just want to stop the bullying and save a child
Because
I SPENT MANY YEARS IN A STUMBLING PLACE

HIV began one person at a time…

And it will end one person at a time…

But it takes two to tango…